Wagner

FOR BEGINNERS

Michael White and Kevin Scott

Edited by Richard Appignanesi

ICON BOOKS

Published in 1995 by Icon Books Ltd.,
52 High Street, Trumpington, Cambridge CB2 2LS

Distributed in the UK, Europe and Asia by the Penguin Group:
Penguin Books Ltd, 27 Wrights Lane, London W8 5TZ

Published in Australia in 1996 by Allen & Unwin Pty. Ltd.,
PO Box 8500, 9 Atchison Street, St. Leonards, NSW 2065

Originating editor: Richard Appignanesi

ISBN 1 874166 27 7

Printed and bound in Great Britain by
The Bath Press, Avon

WAGNER FOR BEGINNERS

'There is Beethoven
and Richard, and
after them, nobody.'

Gustav Mahler

'Wherever one goes, one is plagued
with the question:
what do you think of
Richard Wagner?'

Karl Marx

'Perhaps the greatest genius
that ever lived.' W.H.Auden

'He contaminates
everything
He touches.
/he has made
music sick.'

Friedrich Nietzsche

'Most of us are so
helplessly under the spell
of his greatness that we can do
nothing but go raving about
the theatre in ecstasies
of deluded admiration.'

George Bernard Shaw

'Of all the affected,
sapless, soulless, endless doggerel
of sounds I ever endured, that eternity
of nothing was the deadliest.'

John Ruskin

Whether it is fact or not that Richard Wagner is the subject of more books than anyone in history except Napoleon and Jesus, it is true that no other artist dominates the cultural history of modern times in quite the same way...and it's hard to think of one who inspires such extreme responses:

passionate discipleship

v. passionate abhorrence.

In Israel, Wagner's music is effectively unplayable because of its associations with the **Third Reich**. Rare performances draw public protest, questions in the Knesset.

In Bayreuth, though, Wagner occupies the right-hand throne to God.

Every July and August pilgrims gather from the corners of the earth to pay him homage at the annual festival devoted solely to HIS music. As fanatical as any world religion, it is a genre of hero–worship known as

WAGNEROLATRY.

WHY IS HE SO LOVED/ LOATHED?

1. THE OPERAS

There are 13, of which 10 count among the mightiest artistic achievements ever encompassed by man (or woman)—not to mention overtures, songs, marches, symphonies, chamber music and symphonic poems —

> THEY DEMAND HEAVY RESOURCES, BUDGETS AND VOICES AND ARE STAGGERING ONE-MAN PROJECTS, IN THAT I ALWAYS WROTE MY OWN LIBRETTI*.

Libretto*
The IDEA and story line - often all the lyrics
to an opera or operetta the screenplay and script

Die Feen
Das Liebesverbot
RIENZI
Die Fliegender Hollander
Tannhauser
Lohengrin
Tristan und Isolde
Die Meistersinger von Nuremburg
Das Rheingold
DIE VALKURE
Siegfried
GOTTERDÄMMERUNG
Parsifal

To compare them with **CATHEDRALS** is appropriate ~~~

MARVELS, WUNDERWERKE!
...swooned Thomas Mann...
NO DESCRIPTIONS BETTER FIT THESE AMAZING
MANIFESTATIONS OF ART; AND TO NOTHING ELSE
IN THE WHOLE HISTORY OF ARTISTIC PRODUCTION
ARE THEY MORE APPLICABLE, A FEW
GOTHIC CATHEDRALS ALONE EXCEPTED.

~~~~~because their **scale**

tends usually to

out**size**

2. THE IDEAS...

10 bound volumes of essays and autobiographical writings which, for better or worse, have had a major influence on cultural debate in the 19th and 20th Centuries. Wagner wrote not just about aesthetics but about religion, politics, social reform, science, diet and... race.
He was a dedicated anti-Semite.

Some of his ideas were laughably utopian - not least the theory that the world's ills could be solved by

SHIFTING ITS NORTHERN POPULATIONS TO WARMER CLIMATES WHERE THEY WOULDN'T WANT TO EAT MEAT AND COULD EMBRACE COMPASSIONATE VEGETARIANISM.

Others were more ominous:

Wagner's music may have been hijacked by the Nazis: you can't blame him for the fact that Hitler stole his tunes. But his **ideas** were an outright gift to the Holocaust and take some explaining...as we shall see.

He also…

• forecast **Sigmund Freud's** psychoanalytical investigation of the power of the unconscious (Wagner's operas understood psychology before it was invented)

• explored the significance of myth in art long before the modern anthropologist **Claude Lévi–Strauss;**

• set a new **agenda for the arts** and their role in society that would influence (in some cases positively overwhelm) not only musicians but writers, painters, dramatists for generations on.

It's probably not TOO outrageous to suggest that Wagner actually invented MODERN ART.

WE'LL SEE ABOUT THAT !

3. THE MAN

Wagner was a charismatic figure and made extensive provision for personal immortality, starting with an *AUTOBIOGRAPHICAL SKETCH* at the age of 29 (he began keeping notes at 22), then *A COMMUNICATION TO MY FRIENDS*, and finally *MEIN LEBEN*. These accounts fabricate the **myth** of Wagner as a messianic artist–hero and distort the true facts.

In truth, he was an arrogant, manipulative egocentric who exploited the loyalties of those who admired him and believed his genius placed him beyond the requirements of reasonable behaviour.

THROUGH MY SUFFERINGS AS AN ARTIST I ACQUIRED A SUPERIOR RIGHT THAT RAISED ME FAR, FAR ABOVE THE WORLD AND MADE ME INWARDLY A HALLOWED CREATURE.

What critics make of all this depends on the extent to which his works, ideas and life can be disentangled and considered separately. If nothing else, the lesson of Wagner is that **great artists are not necessarily great human beings** and often need special pleading from their biggest fans.

"I FIND AN ELEMENT OF NAZISM NOT ONLY IN WAGNER'S QUESTIONABLE LITERATURE BUT IN HIS MUSIC AND CREATIVE WORK ... AND EVEN SO I'VE LOVED THAT WORK SO MUCH THAT EVEN TODAY I AM DEEPLY STIRRED WHENEVER IT REACHES MY EAR

Thomas Mann (1875-1955)

THE LIFE: Wagner spent much of it on the run – from creditors, governments and cheated husbands.

He was born in LEIPZIG in 1813 – the same year as his great opera rival Giuseppe Verdi. Anyone around at the time would more likely have remembered 1813 for the defeat of Napoleon at the Battle of Leipzig.

LEIPZIG was a music capital of Europe, famous as the home of J.S.Bach and Felix Mendelssohn. Little Richard was baptized in the Thomaskirche and studied at the Thomasschule where Bach was once the Kantor (choirmaster).

His mother…{Johanna Rosine Wagner née Pätz (1774–1848)} – no doubts here – was a **Fallen Woman**, the former mistress of a minor German aristocrat. When Richard grew up to write operas, it was probably significant that so many of them featured fatherless children…

. . . and men who see the women they adore as mother–figures.

For most of his childhood, he wasn't actually called Richard Wagner but Richard Geyer. To this day, his parentage remains uncertain. His legal father, Carl Wagner, died when he was six months old. He was then adopted with suspicious swiftness by one **Ludwig Geyer**, who may have been the true father all along. In any event, Geyer died when Richard was eight.

Ludwig Geyer (1779-1821)

was an actor and influenced his family accordingly. Five of the seven children in his household ended up professionally involved with THEATRE.
It was Richard's first love. And, starting as he meant to continue, he thought **big**.

At 14 he wrote an epic tragedy...

CONSTRUCTED OUT OF HAMLET ... AND LEAR! FORTY TWO PEOPLE DIED IN THE COURSE OF THIS PIECE AND I WAS FORCED TO BRING MOST OF THEM BACK AS GHOSTS, OTHERWISE I'D HAVE BEEN SHORT OF CHARACTERS FOR MY FINAL ACT

Music was just an adjunct to his dramatic ambitions, and the music teaching he received was scrappy....But then he discovered

Ludwig van   Beethoven

(1770-1827)

who became his obsession and the subject of what he later claimed to be '**ecstatic**' visions. Above all, he was fascinated by the way

Beethoven's 9th Symphony

fused 'pure' orchestral music with poetic texts.

ITS NECESSARY CONSEQUENCE IS NONE OTHER THAN THE *ARTWORK OF THE FUTURE,* TO WHICH BEETHOVEN HAS FORGED THE ARTISTIC KEY

For the rest of his life, he claimed *that* symphony as a determining inspiration for his operas. It was played at the official opening of Bayreuth.

And with the view to history that Wagner always had, he actively promoted the idea of himself as **Beethoven's** natural successor.

Other early influences were the fanciful **MAGIC OPERAS** that featured prominently in the traditions of Viennese theatre. Mozart's **MAGIC FLUTE** (1791) was one, and related stagings of the supernatural like Carl Maria von Weber's **DER FREISCHÜTZ** (1821) and Heinrich Marschner's **DER VAMPYR** (1828).

Immersed in them, Wagner started and abandoned a teenage opera called **DIE HOCHZEIT** (The Marriage).

The British Empire (HQ) ✪ London

Alsace-Lorraine

{France} ✪ Paris

✡ Meyerbeer (1791-1864)

Berlioz (1803/69) ✡ Offenbach (1819/80)

Gounod (1818-93)

Bizet (1838-75)

✡ Saint-Saens (1835-1922)

Zurich

Switzer-land

Franck (1822-90)

Faure (1845-1924)

Debussy (1862-1918)

Marseilles

{Spain}

✪ Madrid

Barcelona

✪

Lisbon

Gibralta

Norway

Sweden

Den-
mark

JS **Bach** (1685-1750)

Handel (1685-1759)

Tchaikovsky
(1840-93)

{Russia}

Gluck (1715-87)

Weber (1786-1826)   ✪ Berlin

Warsaw ✪

Beethoven (1770-1827) *Schumann* (1810-56)

{Germany and Prussia}

{Poland}

Wagner (1813-83) Leipzig

Chopin (1810-49)

✡Mendelssohn (1809-47)

Brahms (1833-97)

Beyreuth

{Austria} ✪Vienna

R.Strauss (1864-1949)

Haydn (1732-1810)

Munich ✪

Mozart (1756-91)

Schubert (1795-1828)

Bruchner (1824-96)

J Strauss (1825-98)

✡Mahler (1860-1911)

{Hungary} Liszt (1811-86)

Salzburg

{Italy}

Rossini (1792-1868)

✪ Milan

Donizetti (1797-1848)

Bellini (1801-35) Venice

Florence

Corsica

Verdi (1813- 1901)

Sardinia

✪ Rome

Naples

Sicily

But the following year, aged 19, his career began in earnest with the first of a succession of jobs that took him through the civil service–like hierarchy of German theatres. Starting as chorus master at the very provincial Würzburg, he shuffled off to Magdeburg, Königsberg, Riga and at the same time was writing the operas of his so-called…

FLEGELJAHRE

…years of awkward cultural adolescence.

There are three FLEGELJAHRE operas…

DIE FEEN, DAS LIEBESVERBOT
and RIENZI.

In 1836, he had married an actress, **_Minna Planner_** *(1809-66)*. The relationship collapsed into a cyclic farce of mutual infidelity, desertion (Minna's first departure came within six months of the marriage) and pursuit across Europe.

In his own life, Wagner found a matchless precedent for all the loveless marriages that feature in his operas.

Dresden
Berlin

RIGA
999km

Würzburg

Bayreuth

Munich

VIENNA

DIE FEEN [THE FAIRIES] (1833/34) is Wagner's first completed opera and a German Romantic fantasy steeped in Weber. Musically it's unremarkable, written in terms that Wagner would soon supersede. But the <u>story</u> introduces three ideas that will return over and again in Wagner's later work…

* QUESTIONS THAT MUST NOT BE ASKED

* REDEMPTION

* TRANSFIGURATION

A mortal falls in love with a fairy and promises not to ask who she is. His curiosity gets the better of him, with the result that he loses her (as in C.W. Gluck's *ORPHEUS AND EURYDICE, 1762* but more importantly in *Wagner's LOHENGRIN, 1848*) and she turns to stone.

But the power of his love proves so great that it rescues her from statuary doom and wins him immortality beside her (as in Mozart's *THE MAGIC FLUTE,* 1791 but also in Wagner's own *THE FLYING DUTCHMAN*).

DAS LIEBESVERBOT

[THE BAN ON LOVE] 1835/36 was Wagner's first opera to reach the stage.
DIE FEEN never made it in his lifetime. It had one disastrous performance, and the opera company thereafter collapsed.

The music this time is *Italianate*. Wagner had recently discovered the *'bel canto'* operas of

Vincenzo Bellini

(1801 -35)

and taken to denouncing the comparative Pedantry of Teutonic style ...

The story, after Shakespeare's **MEASURE FOR MEASURE,** is frivolously comic: a head of state bans love and sexual licence in his land but falls in love himself and is revealed a hypocrite.

But underlying it – and for the first time in Wagner's work – is a philosophical position:

the hedonistic libertarianism of the…

21

YOUNG GERMAN MOVEMENT

which rejected the inhibitions of bourgeois morality in favour of natural freedom and sensual indulgence. A conveniently packaged rationale for his own extramarital adventures, Wagner recycled 'Young German' thinking into his later operas where marriage is usually associated with stagnant relationships in contrast to the ecstasy of less conventional couplings.

RIENZI

(1838/40)

AT THAT HOUR IT BEGAN

RIENZI is a messianic Roman tribune who sacrifices himself to cleanse Rome of its **'degenerate'** nature – an adjective (ENTARTET in German) which would acquire more specific resonance 100 years later in the **Third Reich.**

Adolf Hit ler

saw himself as a RIENZI and traced the beginnings of his struggle to cleanse the world to a performance he attended in 1906.

Among his personal possessions he kept the manuscript full score, which is now lost. Perished, probably, in the ruins of the bunker.

RIENZI is, in its uncut version, the <u>longest</u> of all Wagner's operas: a **Cecil B. de Mille** epic of ancient Rome whose grand processions, crowd scenes, ballets took six hours to get through at the first performance.

It was the first success that made his name throughout Europe.

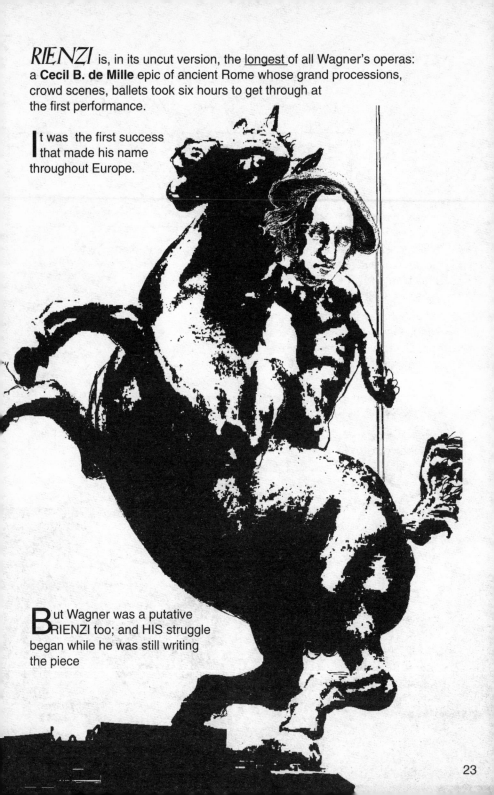

But Wagner was a putative RIENZI too; and HIS struggle began while he was still writing the piece

E ssential to the myth that Wagner fabricated for himself was the idea of the artist–hero whose genius must be indulged at all costs.

Meanwhile, he was sinking into **DEBT**.

... A VORACIOUS, YET UNCOMMONLY TENDER SENSUALITY WHICH MUST BE FLATTERED IF I AM TO ACCOMPLISH THE CRUEL HARDSHIP OF CREATING IN MY MIND A NONEXISTENT WORLD.'

In Wagner's case, the costs were considerable. He adopted the pose of a scented aesthete, draped himself in silks and furs tailored to a pseudo-historical look (hats out of Rembrandt).

In 1863, he hired a Viennese milliner, Bertha Goldwag, who followed him from city to city, smothering his apartments in crushed velvet.

The money to support this sybaritic lifestyle would, Wagner always assumed, be provided by admirers.

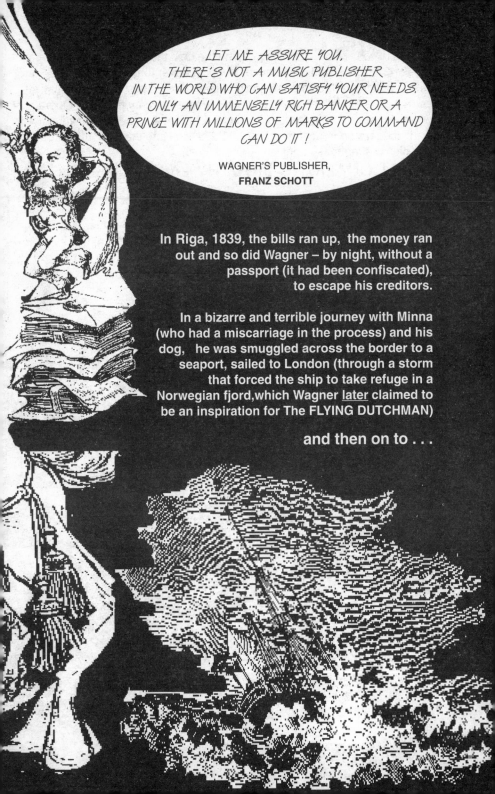

LET ME ASSURE YOU,
THERE'S NOT A MUSIC PUBLISHER
IN THE WORLD WHO CAN SATISFY YOUR NEEDS.
ONLY AN IMMENSELY RICH BANKER OR A
PRINCE WITH MILLIONS OF MARKS TO COMMAND
CAN DO IT!

WAGNER'S PUBLISHER,
FRANZ SCHOTT

In Riga, 1839, the bills ran up, the money ran out and so did Wagner – by night, without a passport (it had been confiscated), to escape his creditors.

In a bizarre and terrible journey with Minna (who had a miscarriage in the process) and his dog, he was smuggled across the border to a seaport, sailed to London (through a storm that forced the ship to take refuge in a Norwegian fjord, which Wagner <u>later</u> claimed to be an inspiration for The FLYING DUTCHMAN)

and then on to . . .

PARIS which proved, during the next three years of living there, (1839/42) to be a Bad Experience he would never forget. In Paris, Wagner was impoverished, on the threshold of imprisonment for debt, and humiliated by persistent failure to get any of his work staged by the Paris Opéra which, in the mid 19th Century, was the centre of the operatic universe. Paris triggered a resentment that would harden into the least attractive qualities of Wagner's later life:

NATIONALISTIC BIGOTRY and ANTI-SEMITISM.

I DO NOT BELIEVE IN ANY OTHER TYPE OF REVOLUTION THAN THAT WHICH BEGINS WITH THE BURNING DOWN OF PARIS .. A CURE BY FIRE TO SYMBOLIZE THE LIBERATION OF THE WORLD FROM ALL THAT'S ROTTEN.

Why anti-Semitism? Because the dominant composer at the Paris Opéra was

GIACOMO MEYERBEER
[1791-1864]

as successful as Wagner wasn't, and **a Jew**. Meyerbeer, in truth, was welcoming and tried to help. But Wagner, looking for something to blame for his predicament, decided the Opéra was subservient to a Jewish conspiracy with Meyerbeer at its head.

HE REMINDS ME OF THE DARKEST – I MIGHT SAY WICKED – PERIOD OF MY LIFE, WHEN HE PRETENDED TO PROTECT ME; A PERIOD OF CONNECTIONS AND BACK-STAIRCASES'.

For the rest of his life, Wagner never tired of denouncing Meyerbeer as the incarnation of all that was corrupt and second – rate in art.

But the fact remains that RIENZI was, in all its grandness, a distinctly Meyerbeerian piece; and although it never made it to the Paris Opéra it was finally accepted by the Dresden Opera in 1842 – which is when his fortunes dramatically (though temporarily) improved. In that year, Wagner had settled in Dresden, whose opera company was less prestigious than the Paris Opéra, and immersed himself in the series of **GERMAN ROMANTIC** operas that span the transition from the FLEGELJAHRE to the great works of the later years: **THE FLYING DUTCHMAN, TANNHÄUSER**

and **LOHENGRIN**

THEIR COMMON FACTOR IS THAT THEY DERIVE FROM GERMAN MYTH. OR FROM MATERIAL THAT LOOKS LIKE GERMAN MYTH...

...THE KEY THEMES:

WANDERING,

REDEMPTION

and

TRANSFIGURATION

ARE ALL QUINTESSENTIALLY *WAGNERIAN.*

THE FLYING DUTCHMAN (1840/41)

is his first work of unquestionable genius. Musically it's a conventional grand opera of its time. But it signals Wagner's growing interest in the INNER rather than OUTER LIVES of his characters. Wagner wrote it during his bad (destitute) years in Paris and so he keenly identified with the sufferings of the Dutchman.

The story is actually a British legend set originally in Scotland – which is where the opera was located until just before the première (Dresden, 1843) when everything shifted to Norway.

The Dutchman is an accursed sailor condemned to travel the sea forever, or until he finds the love of a faithful woman.

This turns out to be Senta, a young Norwegian of such utter faithfulness that she throws herself into the sea as a redemptive gesture of self-sacrifice.

Result: the lovers are united in heavenly bliss.

TANNHÄUSER (1842/45)

is true German myth, set in an idealized Middle Ages and celebrating an ideal of pure, chaste love that Wagner intermittently upheld in art, if not in real life.

TANNHÄUSER is a knight, torn between the bacchanalian revels of the Venusberg, where love reigns free and steamy,

and the adoring Elisabeth who waits faithfully for him at home.

For his dalliance on the Venusberg even the Pope cannot forgive him. But Elisabeth buys his redemption with her own life: a sacrifice so powerful that it kills Tannhäuser too.

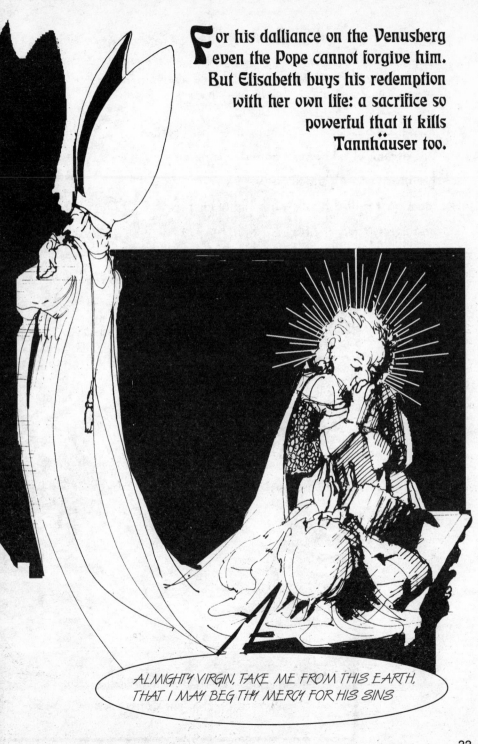

ALMIGHTY VIRGIN, TAKE ME FROM THIS EARTH, THAT I MAY BEG THY MERCY FOR HIS SINS

LOHENGRIN (1845/48) is the link between Wagner the

German Romantic and Wagner the mature composer of **"music drama"** as the later works came to be called. Again, it inhabits a mythical medieval German world.

Elsa has been accused of murdering her brother. She dreams of a knight who will champion her innocence. **M**iraculously he arrives (on a boat pulled by a swan), fights for her, and agrees to marry her,

on condition that she <u>doesn't</u> ask who he is.

Tempted by the malevolent Ortrud, Elsa succumbs to curiosity on her wedding night.
The answer: he is **LOHENGRIN, knight of the Holy Grail** and having revealed his identity he must leave.

The marriage is over, and the swan comes to collect him.

But in another, parting miracle the swan is revealed to be Elsa's brother under a spell cast by **Ortrud**.

Elsa collapses, lifeless, as **LOHENGRIN** departs.

Before *LOHENGRIN* reached its intended premiere in Dresden, the biggest crisis yet in Wagner's life intervened and he was driven out of Germany, to remain in exile for the next 12 years.

It was <u>1848</u>, and in Europe that meant,

REVOLUTION!!!

Political unrest had simmered in the background of Wagner's life since he was a child, growing up in a Europe and a Germany whose internal boundaries had just been redetermined–not very securely– after the defeat of Napoleon. Every tremor in France registered throughout the Continent.

When revolution broke out in Dresden in 1849, Wagner was involved, issuing anarchist tracts and distributing hand–-grenades. **A warrant was issued for his arrest.**

I BECAME A REVOLUTIONARY, AND DECIDED THAT EVERY ASPIRING HUMAN BEING SHOULD CONCERN HIMSELF EXCLUSIVELY WITH POLITICS.

The direction of Wagner's politics was never very clear. But he certainly fell under the influence of the Russian anarchist **Mikhail Bakunin** *(1814-76)*, a rival of **Karl Marx**. Wagner probably never read Marx's **Communist Manifesto** (published in 1848) but the fundamentals of radical socialism certainly coloured his thinking.

He gathered up his wife, dog and parrot, and fled – first to Weimar, to squeeze some money from...

Franz Liszt (1811-86)

whom he' d first met in 1840. Liszt was a 'pop star' of his day, a world–famous virtuoso pianist and a composer of influential '**symphonic poems**'.

SOMETHING TELLS ME I SHOULD LOCK UP COSIMA

He also had two daughters; one called Cosima, twelve years old at the time, was going to figure very large in Richard's life later on...

Wagner carried on to Paris and then Zurich.

The next four years in Zurich were a chasm in Wagner's life in which **HE WROTE NO MUSIC**. He just thought and published an extraordinary series of THEORETICAL ESSAYS which declare his position on every political, cultural and social issue of conceivable relevance to the ills of mid-19th Century Europe.

ART and REVOLUTION (1849)

THE ARTWORK OF THE FUTURE (1849)

JUDAISM IN MUSIC (1850)

OPERA and DRAMA (1851)

A COMMUNICATION TO MY FRIENDS (1851)

These are clumsily written, inconsistent, speciously Utopian, and tend to back their arguments with <u>distorted readings of history</u>. But the arguments themselves are fascinating and proved durably – if not dangerously – **influential**. They address three basic issues:

GERMANY IN CRISIS , THE WORLD IN CRISIS , ART IN CRISIS

and find a common cause…PHILISTINE JEWISH – INSPIRED MATERIALISM
…and a common solution:

REVOLUTION (again)

The '**GERMAN CRISIS**' was that Germany existed more in concept than in actuality. There had never been a single united 'Germany', only a Holy Roman Empire divided between several hundred princes and city–states, reduced to a loose confederation of 39 by the Congress of Vienna (1815), each one fiercely guarding its own territory.

The poet *Friedrich Schiller* (1759-1805) was proclaiming German consciousness in 1802...

A MORAL ENTITY, DWELLING IN THE CULTURE AND CHARACTER OF THE NATION, INDEPENDENT OF ALL POLITICAL ADVENTURING.

But half a century on, nationalism was still regarded as politically subversive.

When *DEUTSCHLAND ÜBER ALLES* (music by Haydn; later the German National anthem) was first sung in 1841, the German princes banned it.

PLAY THE MARSEILLESE!!

BUT HAYDN'S AUSTRIAN!

BOO!

The intensity of Wagner's nationalism varied throughout his life, depending on the changing sources of his income. Financially beholden to the King of Bavaria in the 1860s, he was unsurprisingly Bavarian in outlook. But from the time of his immersion in Romantic medievalism in the 1840s, his operas embodied the

German spirit

with a vengeance, and take much of their tone from the ideology of…

Johann Gottlieb Fichte

(1762–1814),
founder of the nationalistic culture that fed through to the successive German Reichs.

As Wagner grew older, his identification with national culture grew fiercer.

The philosopher

Friedrich Nietzsche *(1844-1900)*

a one–time ardent admirer of Wagner, who turned fiercely against him, noted dryly. . .

IT IS SIGNIFICANT THAT THE ARRIVAL OF WAGNER COINCIDES WITH THE ARRIVAL OF THE REICH, FOR BOTH REQUIRE THE SAME THING. . . OBEDIENCE AND LONG LEGS.

I AM THE MOST GERMAN BEING. I AM THE GERMAN SPIRIT!

THE MASTERSINGERS ends with a grand invocation of 'Holy **German** Art'.

SWEPT INTO PATRIOTIC FERVOUR BY THE FRANCO-PRUSSIAN WAR, I CELEBRATED THE FRENCH DEFEAT BY SENDING BISMARK A HYMN FOR THE CROWNING OF WILHELM I AT VERSAILLES:

''THE PROUDEST CROWN ON EARTH, AS STOLEN FROM US, SHALL UPON HIS HEAD REWARD HIS HOLY DEEDS''.

What, though, was the true role of an artist in all this?

The poet **Heinrich Heine** (1797-1856) supplied Wagner with an answer. Heine was a major influence on Wagner: he wrote poems on *Tannhäuser, Valkyries* and *the Flying Dutchman* long before Wagner took the subjects on.

The name of the last opera in the RING cycle, Götterämmerung,

(Twilight of the Gods) comes from Heine too.

THAT'S ALL GOOD, GERMAN STUFF. . . BUT HEINE WAS IN FACT A JEW

But he also alerted  Wagner to the possibility of a relationship between **ART, MYTH and REVOLUTION;** and the theory Wagner produced as a result was this:

1. GERMANY'S TROUBLES WERE PART OF A UNIVERSAL MALAISE CAUSED BY THE FACT THAT THE WORLD HAD ITS PRIORITIES WRONG.

2. IT WAS ENSLAVED BY BOURGEOIS MATERIALISM AND INSTITUTIONS (LIKE MARRIAGE) THAT REDUCE EVERYTHING TO PROPERTY AND UTILITY, AND INHIBIT THE FREE EXCHANGE OF LOVE.

3. THE WAY TO CHANGE THE WORLD'S PRIORITIES WAS THROUGH ART, AND THAT MEANT REASSERTING THE LOST CENTRALITY OF ART WITHIN SOCIETY.

IN THE ANCIENT CLASSICAL WORLD, ART HAD RITUAL SIGNIFICANCE AS A CELEBRATION OF LIFE. IT INVOLVED THE WHOLE COMMUNITY. AND IT CAME IN THE FORM OF GREAT MULTI-DISCIPLINARY OBSERVANCES THAT EMBRACED MUSIC, VISUAL DRAMA, POETRY AND DANCE.

BUT THE ARRIVAL OF CHRISTIANITY ENCOURAGED PEOPLE TO LOOK BEYOND LIFE, TO AN ENVISAGED OTHER-WORLDLY BLISS. THUS, ART WAS DOWNGRADED INTO ENTERTAINMENT. OPERA IS NOW AN ARTICLE OF FASHION. THE PUBLIC HAVE NO NEED FOR IT; THEY ONLY WANT TO BE DIVERTED.

YAWN

There had to be a new kind of art, delivered by an artist–hero (Wagner himself) and capable of application to the needs of a corrupt world like an **epic therapy**.

IT WOULD BE A REGENERATIVE ARTWORK OF THE FUTURE BUILT FROM THE "FREE ARTISTIC FELLOWSHIP" OF THE VOLK, THE PEOPLE... A *GESAMTKUNSTWERK* OR TOTAL ART FORM, INTEGRATING THE WHOLE RANGE OF CREATIVE AND PERFORMANCE SKILLS — MUSIC, DRAMA, DANCE, SPECTACLE — LIKE THE THEATRE OF THE ANCIENT GREEKS...

AND, ALSO LIKE THEIR THEATRE, BASED ON EPIC MYTHS THAT GAVE IT UNIVERSAL SIGNIFICANCE BEYOND ALL BOUNDARIES OF TIME AND PLACE.

IT'S A LOVELY DRESS... AND IT GOES SO WELL WITH THIS OPERA

45

And what then?, Wagner thought...

LIFT—OFF! !! ...A MIGHTY, *VOLKISH* ORGASM INITIATED BY THE MASTER'S OWN HAND.

IN THE PROCESS OF CIVILIZATION, THE CONSTRAINTS OF WHAT IS NATURAL GROW TO SUCH VAST PROPORTIONS THAT THERE BUILDS UP IN CRUSHED BUT INDESTRUCTIBLE NATURE, THE PRESSURE TO CAST THEM OFF WITH A SINGLE VIOLENT GESTURE.

THE EMPLOYMENT OF THIS STRENGTH IS *REVOLUTION*, AND IT IS THE SPECIFIC TASK OF *ART* TO REVEAL TO THIS SOCIAL FORCE ITS OWN NOBLEST IMPORT AND ITS TRUE DIRECTION.

?

WHERE DO THE JEWS COME INTO ALL THIS?

ER.. NOWHERE.

BECAUSE JUDAISM HAS IN ONE FORM OR ANOTHER BEEN *ERADICATED* IN THE BLAST OF THE ERUPTION.

B ut was this to be a **destruction** of Jews as human beings or of 'Jewishness' as a behaviour pattern? How far did 19th Century German anti-Semites consider Judaism an issue of **biology** rather than **culture**? It isn't always clear.

But certainly there were 'liberals' among them who believed that Jews could be redeemed by renouncing their cultural background, and who accordingly supported the campaign for Jewish emancipation.

For example, the close friend and novelist

Heinrich Laube   *(1806-84)*:

Either we must be barbarians and root out the Jews to the last man, or we must assimilate them.

Laube influenced Wagner's views on the Jewish Question, which hardened around 1848/50 and finally appeared in **JUDAISM IN MUSIC**, one of the key documents in the modern history of anti-Semitism, which Wagner initially published under the pseudonym

K. Freigedank

(= free thought) in 1850.

a common prejudice

It seems hard to square Wagner the libertarian revolutionary with Wagner the anti-Semite. But in the cultural context of his time, the two positions raised no necessary conflict. In fact, many of the most influential revolutionary propagandists in 19th Century Germany targeted Jews as an enemy class, on the grounds that Jewish money propped up the bourgeois-capitalist establishment.

The radical philosopher *Jakob Fries* in 1816 called for...

EXTERMINATION OF THIS JEWISH COMMERCIAL CASTE

...while *Karl Marx's* **Essay on the Jewish Question** (1844) accused the Jews of being

AGENTS OF CAPITALISM.

A nd certainly, there was a visible economic alliance between wealthy Jews and the German princes. So when the princes crushed the risings of 1848/49 and the cause of Unification seemed lost, the Jews came under verbal fire as counter-revolutionaries: **ENEMIES OF FREEDOM.** And THAT idea acquired a supra-economic resonance from the earlier writings of *Immanuel Kant (1724-1804)* who argued that the Jews were an enslaved race, locked in their own past and loveless…

. . A NATION OF USURERS. . .BOUND BY SUPERSTITION . . .OUTWITTING THE PEOPLE WHO SHELTER THEM.

The question remained, what to do about them. The political dramatist *Karl Gutzkow (1811-78)* had no doubt . .

JUDAISM HAD OUTLIVED ITS TIME. ITS FUNCTION FINISHED WITH CHRISTIANITY. ALL THAT REMAINED FOR IT WAS "SELBSTVERNICHTUNG" – SELF-DESTRUCTION..

This term found its way into Wagner's own language.

SELBSTVERNICHTUNG,.....YES, I LIKE THE <u>RING</u> OF THAT!

JUDAISM MU

What is Wagner's big problem with "Jews in music"? Here is his assessment of the composer *Felix Mendelssohn*

MENDELSSOHN SHOWS US THAT A JEW CAN HAVE THE RICHEST ABUNDANCE OF TALENTS AND BE A MAN OF THE BROADEST YET MOST REFINED CULTURE, THE HIGHEST, IRREPROACHABLE INTEGRITY, BUT STILL INCAPABLE OF SUPPLYING THE PROFOUND, HEART-SEIZING, SOUL-SEARCHING EXPERIENCE WE EXPECT FROM ART.

In other words, Jewish art (Mendelssohn's or Meyerbeer's and all things the crowds cheered at the Paris Opèra) was a confection of surface charm:

"EFFECTS WITHOUT CAUSES".

Jews, for Wagner, kept art harnessed to the mediocrity of entertainment, using it as a means to ingratiate themselves with the host societies in which they lived.

THE ATTEMPTS OF JEWS TO MAKE ART HAVE INVARIABLY THE PROPERTY OF COLDNESS, OF NON-INVOLVEMENT, TO THE POINT OF BEING TRIVIAL AND RIDICULOUS. WE ARE BOUND TO CATEGORIZE THE JEWISH PERIOD IN MODERN MUSIC AS A TIME OF CONSUMMATE STAGNATION'.

THE "JEWISH PERIOD" IN MUSIC? WHAT IS HE TALKING ABOUT?

You would think from listening to Wagner that Jews <u>dominated</u> music in his day. He makes them out to be far more powerful than is numerically justified.

Something else is bothering Wagner— And it looks suspiciously like popularity— the envy of one freelance composer for the success of others.

The Era of Emancipation and Self Promotion

Musicians and composers up to Beethoven's time had been *employees* of the nobility and the Church. This system of patronage bred dependence but also some security. The new figure of the musician to emerge after the Napoleonic period was the *freelance virtuoso* who catered for a mass audience. Performers and composers like the violinist

Niccolo Paganini *(1782-1840)*

and the pianist *Franz Liszt (1811-84)*

were immensely charismatic entertainers with retinues of swooning females...

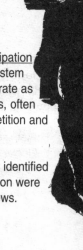

YOUR SUCCESS DEPENDS ON PUTTING (SHAPELY) BUMS ON SEATS!!

...the forerunners of modern Pop stars like Elvis Presley and Mick Jagger. Chopin and Mendelssohn were two other enigmatic "superstars".

A new era of <u>cultural emancipation</u> had begun, a free market system in which artists have to operate as self-promoting entrepreneurs, often in conditions of fierce competition and insecurity.

And the people most closely identified with free market emancipation were (who else, of course) the Jews.

Wagner too was a freelance 'entrepreneur'. An example of the competition he faced occurred in 1858, a year before he completed *Tristan and Isolde*. That year saw the première of a smash hit comic opera by

Jacques Offenbach

(1819-80)

Orpheus in the Underworld.

Which gave us a tune still familiar today for its high-kicking Can-Can dance, immortalized by posters of the Moulin Rouge.

INCIDENTALLY WASN'T OFFENBACH JEWISH?

It begins to look as though **'Jewishness'** is Wagner's shorthand for mass popular entertainment and a scapegoat symbol of EVERYTHING that his own sincerely revolutionary art struggled to overcome and replace.

While his own concept of MUSIC DRAMA was developing, there swept through Europe, by way of his loathed Paris, a craze for frothy, superficial romps which threatened to undermine 'serious' music and its ideals.

Wagner against history...

All those theorizing Zurich essays, with their suspect core of anti-Semitism, were leading Wagner towards his greatest stage works: PARSIFAL, TRISTAN AND ISOLDE, THE MASTERSINGERS, and THE RING. These are the 'artworks of the future' Wagner offered as his cultural salvation of the world.

He never called them operas: opera was the Meyerbeerian entertainment of the old regime. He called them dramas – or, as history prefers to name them, **MUSIC DRAMAS**. They were intended to surpass all operatic precedents in

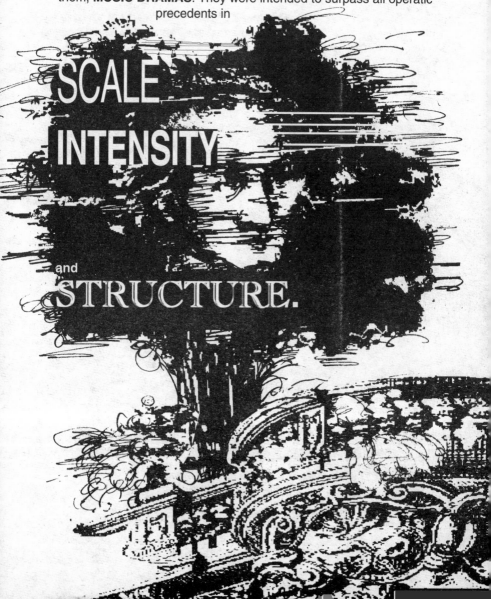

SCALE

INTENSITY

and
STRUCTURE.

Wagner's mature "MUSIC DRAMAS" break away radically from the standard practice of traditional opera with its compartmental divisions of RECITATIVE, ARIA, ENSEMBLE, CHORUS – and that most Parisian of prerequisites…DANCE. With choruses as they were known, and the ever 'incidental' ballet, eliminated, Wagner, in his greatest operas, draws those elements into a vast unity of commentary and confrontation. Lavish, though his music is, the 'narrative' focus is on one profound statement at a time. And often a very long time, indeed.

MONSIEUR WAGNER A DES BEAUX MOMENTS, MAIS DES MAUVAIS QUART D'HEURES

Gioacchino Rossini   (1792/1868)

who dominated the Parisian music 'scene' was a transitional composer who helped to pave the way for Wagner's innovations. Famed for his comic operas, he developed not only the *bel canto* repertory but grand histories, mixing myth with fact, like *William Tell*, which in its vast scale alone seems Wagnerian.

Rossini was as influential for his **Salons** as for his own composition. At these meetings were gathered writers, painters and composers of the day. At such occasions Wagner would have met many of the great artists of his day.

Endless Melody and the Leitmotiv

Wagner replaced the established <u>entertainment</u> components of opera with long, seamless, open-ended expanses of music that he called…

UNENDLICHE MELODIE
.. ENDLESS MELODY ...

ITS ENDLESSNESS
DID NOT APPEAL
TO EVERY
LISTENER

In the absence of the normal structural forms of opera, Wagner's problem was to give his audience aural landmarks that would guide them through the long stretches of writing and provide a sense of unifying shape to what they heard. They also needed periodic wake-up calls to summon their attention during long stretches of theatre where <u>very little happens</u> in terms of <u>EXTERNAL action</u>.

The drama of these works is principally INTERNAL, about emotions rather than events; and Wagner allows plenty of time for the emotions to register, against what is often an unchanging stage picture of characters who stand and sing each other monologues.

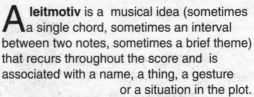

The solution was the 'Leitmotiv'

(guiding theme)

A **leitmotiv** is a musical idea (sometimes a single chord, sometimes an interval between two notes, sometimes a brief theme) that recurs throughout the score and is associated with a name, a thing, a gesture or a situation in the plot. A kind of signature tune, a **leitmotiv** might announce something on stage. More subtly, it might suggest that somebody on stage is thinking of that thing. And always it provides a means for the music (very often, the orchestra) to ENTER the story, enriching its textural depth with an added layer of commentary.

There are **leitmotivs** of sorts in Wagner's earlier work, but it wasn't until THE RING that they became an essential tool of his trade, interwoven with a systematic thoroughness that literally knits the score together. Scholars have identified more than 100 motifs in THE RING , and attached titles to them like

The Rhine,

Alberich's curse,

Wotan's spear.

The orchestra itself no longer serves merely as a "big guitar" accompanying the singers' tuneful antics on stage, but is now fused with the drama itself as an essential part of the characters' expression, actions and even thought processes.

In fact the orchestra becomes more than a music-making body, It literally takes an integral part of the dramatic plot structure.

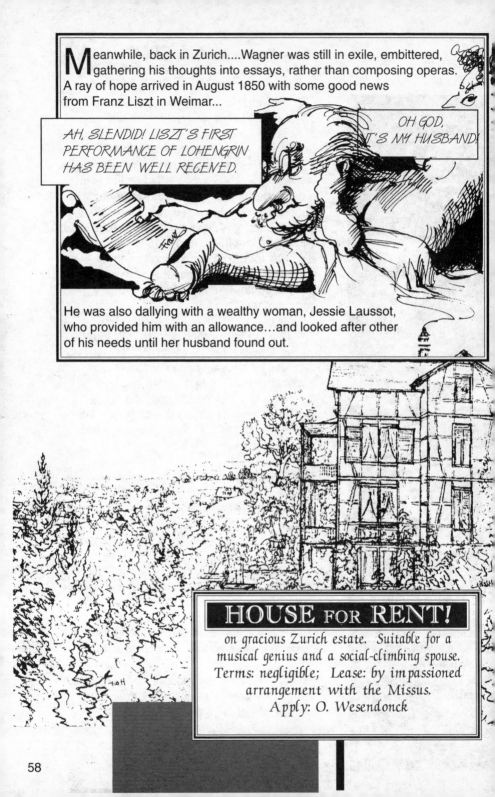

Meanwhile, back in Zurich....Wagner was still in exile, embittered, gathering his thoughts into essays, rather than composing operas. A ray of hope arrived in August 1850 with some good news from Franz Liszt in Weimar...

AH, SLENDID! LISZT'S FIRST PERFORMANCE OF LOHENGRIN HAS BEEN WELL RECEIVED.

OH GOD, IT'S MY HUSBAND!

He was also dallying with a wealthy woman, Jessie Laussot, who provided him with an allowance…and looked after other of his needs until her husband found out.

HOUSE FOR RENT!

on gracious Zurich estate. Suitable for a musical genius and a social-climbing spouse. Terms: negligible; Lease: by impassioned arrangement with the Missus.
Apply: O. Wesendonck

In 1852 he met Otto and Mathilde Wesendonck, a new–rich bourgeois couple living in a grand classical villa on a hill outside the city.

!!!THE WESENDONCK AFFAIR!!!

Over the next few years their friendship grew, as did Wagner's debts; and he persuaded Otto Wesendonck to pay off his creditors.

He also moved – with Minna, who was still, periodically, around – into a house adjoining the Wesendonck estate.

And there, under the noses of their respective spouses, Wagner and Mathilde began a passionate – albeit 'platonic' – relationship.

59

A setting of Mathilde's verse –
the WESENDONCK LIEDER –
gave Wagner an excuse to spend a lot of time alone with Mathilde.
More importantly, the Wesendonck Lieder became
a trial study for the pinnacle of Wagnerism…

TRISTAN AND ISOLDE (1854/5a9)

Tristan is a Cornish knight in legendary times. **Isolde** is his captive: he is bringing her by sea from Ireland back to Cornwall where she'll be required, against her will, to marry Tristan's uncle **King Marke**.

On the way, she tries to kill him, and herself, with poison. But instead of dying they fall crazily into each other's arms. It wasn't poison after all, but a love-draught (cleverly switched by Brangäne, Isolde's handmaid).

At King Marke's court they meet secretly by night, but are discovered. There's a fight, Tristan is wounded, and his broken body is removed to France where he waits - slowly, painfully and barrenly - to die.

A *ship arrives, it is Isolde;*
they are passionately reunited. But he still dies.
And Isolde joins him, ecstatically transfigured in what Wagner calls

. . . a *Liebestod* . (Love—death)

Tristan was an attempt to recreate in music as never before (and hardly ever since) the erotic charge of heightened sexual passion.

The latter–day American composer Virgil Thomson claimed to hear, implicit in the score,

...THE SOUND OF TRISTAN AND ISOLDE SIMULTANEOUSLY EJACULATING SEVEN TIMES.

And that was just Act II! As Wagner wrote to Liszt...

'Since I've never enjoyed the real happiness of love, I want to build a monument to this most beautiful of dreams in which love will be thoroughly sated from start to finish...

For a 19th Century audience, TRISTAN was an X–CERTIFICATE experience: an unprecedented example of the power of music to suggest,

A nd for 20th Century audiences it can be the same. Because TRISTAN represents in its most concentrated form the subversive quality in Wagner's work which, now as then, seems capable of penetrating the subconscious of his listeners and addressing buried feelings. In the words of the distinguished Wagner commentator Bryan Magee,

IT GETS PAST THE CENSOR.

. . .Much as Wagner knew it would.

W hen he was working on the score he saw himself as locked into the process of unleashing on the world some awesome Frankensteinian creation.

THIS TRISTAN IS TURNING INTO SOMETHING FEARFUL! THAT LAST ACT!!! I'M AFRAID THE OPERA WILL BE FORBIDDEN — UNLESS THE WHOLE THING IS TURNED INTO A PARODY BY BAD PRODUCTION: ONLY MEDIOCRE PERFORMANCES CAN SAVE ME! COMPLETELY GOOD ONES ARE BOUND TO DRIVE PEOPLE MAD

Technically, the luscious, perfumed atmosphere of the opera is derived from heavily chromatic writing: sliding semitonal shifts through sharps and flats that stretch to the limit the established convention of organizing music around recognizable key centres. And the whole sound world of the piece is miraculously summarized in the opening chord – the 'TRISTAN chord' which must be the most exhaustively debated and profoundly influential group of four notes ever put to paper.

20th Century music starts
– some fifty years before its time –
with these notes as they ease seductively
from one cushioned discord to another.

This chord establishes the governing *Leitmotiv of the Love-Potion*, which is central to the story and a symbol of the irresistibility of sexual desire however forbidding the circumstances.
Given Wagner's own circumstances, it was a consoling notion.

Apart from Mathilde Wesendonck, inspiration for the opera came from the philosophy of

Arthur Schopenhauer (1788-1860)

which Wagner first read in 1854 and claimed to be the most momentous discovery of his life.

...A GIFT FROM HEAVEN FOR ME IN MY SOLITUDE. HIS REASONING IS TERRIBLY STERN, BUT IN IT ALONE IS SALVATION..

Thereafter Shopenhauer's philosophy was his abiding obsession, incorporated into all his MUSIC–DRAMAS.
He made repeated attempts to befriend the author, who ignored them.

OUT TO LUNCH!!!

A. Schopenhauer
Pessimist

*I DID NOT ADMIRE WAGNERIAN OPERA...
...I PREFERRED ROSSINI AND THOUGHT NO OPERA SHOULD BE MORE THAN TWO HOURS LONG.*

The two men never met.

But Schopenhauer did venerate music and accorded it a central function in his world view.

THE OTHER ARTS SPEAK ONLY OF THE SHADOW,
BUT MUSIC SPEAKS OF THE ESSENCE OF THINGS -
ALL THE FEELINGS OF OUR INNERMOST EXPERIENCE.
IT DOES NOT DEPICT PHENOMENA, BUT IS THE DIRECT
EXPRESSION OF THE WILL ITSELF.

Schopenhauer's was not the happiest philosophy.
In fact it was the bleakest possible view of life —
partly derived from Buddhism, partly from Aristotle
—which taught that we can only resign ourself to suffering
in a world where everything we consider 'real'
is mere surface illusion. Schopenhauer's key text
THE WORLD AS WILL AND REPRESENTATION (1818)
opens with his basic principle:

Schopenhauer's 'Will' is the universal life–force inherent in all beings that drives us on – through 'struggle, jostling crowds, shortages, misery and fear' from which our only hope of relief is an ascetic surrender:

RENUNCIATION!!

'The world is my idea.'

YES, THAT'S IT... THE WORLD IS MY IDEA!!!

Schopenhauer also provided Wagner with the idea that the human sex drive was itself part of the Will, and therefore something else to which we might as well yield. Schopenhauer, of course, was negative on love. Like everything else, it would end in tears.

But Wagner's absorption of Schopenhauer was, for all its enthusiasm, selective; and he adjusted the reasoning to his own ends.

Renouncing life
for love = salvation.

Some years later, when Wagner read Darwin's **ORIGIN OF SPECIES**, he found support for his adjustment of Schopenhauer to more optimistic possibilities.

SEXUAL WILL WAS THE DETERMINING FORCE IN NATURAL SELECTION...

...AND THEREFORE PART OF THE PROCESS WHEREBY HUMANITY WAS SAVED FOR THE FUTURE.

Schopenhauer also embellished Wagner's anti–Semitism. Judaism was a false religion in that it encouraged resistance to the Will. It knew nothing of the resignation and COMPASSION (*Mitleid*) that were the ennobling qualities of suffering humanity.

IT IS A PERNICIOUS MYTH THAT CHRISTIANITY WAS RELATED TO JUDAISM.

THE NEW TESTAMENT MUST SOMEHOW BE OF INDIAN ORIGIN . . .

— EVERYTHING THAT IS TRUE IN CHRISTIANITY IS FOUND IN BUDDHISM AND BRAHMINISM.

The Aryanization of Christianity was a proposition Wagner fervently supported.

ONE OF THE MOST TERRIBLE CONFUSIONS OF WORLD HISTORY WAS THAT JESUS HAD COME TO BE IDENTIFIED WITH JEWRY

The brew of borrowed philosophy and personal experience that poured into TRISTAN reached perfection when Wagner had to renounce his love for Mathilde.
They had been found out; and after terrible exchanges between Minna, the Wesendoncks and himself, Wagner packed his bags and left for Venice in August 1858, only to be moved on by the ruling Austrian authorities as a fugitive from German justice.

He returned to Switzerland, finished *TRISTAN* in Lucerne, and then moved again to. . .er. . .**Paris,** where he attempted another assault on the Paris Opéra with a revised version of *Tannhäuser.*

PARIS WAS ANOTHER BAD EXPERIENCE. . . I WAS SO KEEN FOR A PRODUCTION THERE THAT I ENLARGED THE OPENING SCENE, AGAINST MY PRINCIPALS. . .

After 163 rehearsals (the performers found it difficult) the opening night was disrupted by members of the Jockey Club making dog-noises because they objected to the fact that the ballet came in Act I. "Fashionable" French audiences only came to opera for the dancing it incorporated, and rarely arrived at the theatre before Act II.

The 2nd night was similarly disrupted. On the 3rd, there were riots in the auditorium. There never was a 4th night. The production was withdrawn.

Such were the conditions in which 19th Century composers worked.

Minna followed him to Paris in yet another attempt to save the marriage and, according to Wagner's instructions, arrived complete with dog and parrot........

...IT DIDN'T WORK, AND I FINALLY LEFT RICHARD IN 1861!

With – at last – an amnesty in his pocket, Wagner returned to Germany where he was visited by th conductor **Hans von Bülow**, (1830-94) a devotee of his music, who later conducted the premièrs of *Tristan* and *The Mastersingers*. Von Bulow had studied with Liszt and, as a result, married Liszt's daughter, **Cosima**.

On that fateful visit, in July 1862, von Bulow brought his wife with him. She was still in her mid – twenties.

WITHIN A YEAR COSIMA AND I WERE LOVERS, COMMITTED TO EACH OTHER..

. . . WITH SOBS AND TEARS'.

Meanwhile, his debts were accumulating, again, and a warrant issued for his arrest, again. He needed a miracle. And right on cue it surfaced in the form of....**Ludwig,** who is famous (a) for being mad (b) for building the original Walt Disney fairy castle, Neuschwanstein (c) for being the most dedicated **patron** in the history of music.

When Ludwig came to the Bavarian throne in 1864, he was 18, gay, not wholly sane, and infatuated with Wagner's operas to the point of being in love with their author. One of his first acts as king was to summon Wagner to Munich and promise:

The mean cares of everyday life I will banish from you forever. I will procure for you the peace you have longed for. . . . Oh how I have looked forward to the time when I could do this! I hardly dared indulge myself in the hope of so quickly being able to prove my love to you.

Wagner was installed in a royal villa, his debts were paid out of the roya[l] exchequer, and in return he played up to the royal affections.

HE SENDS FOR ME ONCE OR TWICE A D[AY] I THEN FLY TO HIM AS A LOVER THUS WE [...] FOR HOURS, LOST IN EACH OTHER'S GAZE[...]

Rumours in fact circulated that Wagner and Ludwig WERE lovers, although the truth is that Wagner was by now cohabiting with Cosi[ma] and she was pregnant with their first child.
He assured the king that she was merely an **'amanuensis'**.

After further raids on the exchequer to keep Wagner's creditors at bay, the scandal broke. For Ludwig it became a political crisis, undermining his authority and activating a chain of events that ultimately lost him his throne and his life. Still he continued to finance Wagner in exile, and paid for a house at Lucerne called **'Tribschen'** where Wagner settled in 1866.

Bertha Goldwag followed with the pink satin furnishings, and Cosima von Bülow with the children:

> TWO FROM MY MARRIAGE WITH HANS, AND MY FIRST, ISOLDE, FROM MY ARTISTIC COMMUNION WITH RICHARD

Wagner's children were always named after characters in whichever opera he was writing at the time: hence…

Isolde. . .Eva. . .Siegfried.

....For photographs, he liked to dress them up as their originals.

A less welcome arrival at Tribschen was Ludwig himself, who turned up unexpectedly on Wagner's birthday, dressed as another of Wagner's characters, Walther, the hero-knight of THE MASTERSINGERS.

...DEAR FRIEND, I'LL GIVE UP MY THRONE AND COME TO LIVE WITH YOU AT TRIBSCHEN.!

Wagner, horrified, dissuaded him.

THE MASTERSINGERS OF NUREMBERG (1861/67)

was Wagner's new project, and very different from TRISTAN.
It was• **a comedy** (so Wagner insisted), • **realistic** (as opposed to mythic)
• **bourgeois-domestic** (as against epic-heroic) • **busy with external action**
(rather than a static drama of internalized emotions)• **more conventional as
music** (no one could say modernity began with MASTERSINGERS) • **with an
overtly political statement** of German nationalism in the final scene
which the Third Reich **later** commandeered as a set–piece entertainment for the
Nazi party rallies at NUREMBERG.

The story is Wagner's own, although with details borrowed from the great
poet *J.W. von Goethe* (1749-1832) and *Gustav Lortzing* (1801-51)
and the introduction of historical characters.

Essentially, it's a benign and radiant piece but with a potentially darker
subtext; and modern readings depend on the extent to which the
subtext can be ignored, excused, or otherwise explained away.

It happens in 16th Century NUREMBERG where social life centres on trade guilds, not least the guild of MASTERSINGERS who take pride in the craft of song-making according to traditional rules.

Pogner's

achs Shoes

One of the Mastersingers, **Pogner**, has a daughter, **Eva** who is promised in marriage to the winner of a song contest. She is loved by a young knight, **Walther**, who wants to enter the contest. But the song he sings as a test of entry proves too radical, too heedless of the rules, to be accepted.

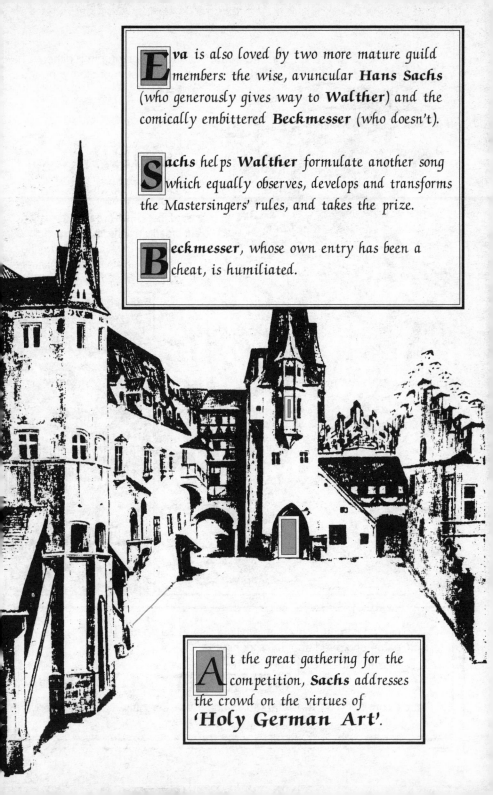

Eva is also loved by two more mature guild members: the wise, avuncular **Hans Sachs** (who generously gives way to **Walther**) and the comically embittered **Beckmesser** (who doesn't).

Sachs helps **Walther** formulate another song which equally observes, develops and transforms the Mastersingers' rules, and takes the prize.

Beckmesser, whose own entry has been a cheat, is humiliated.

At the great gathering for the competition, **Sachs** addresses the crowd on the virtues of **'Holy German Art'**.

And Schopenhauer is not forgotten either . . . Sachs has a celebrated monologue on the subject of

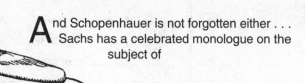

WAHN

a word that defies precise translation but broadly means 'illusion' or 'folly'. Sachs sees folly all around him: the bogus realities that Schopenhauer identifies as governing our lives.

But once again, it's Schopenhauer—adjusted to admit the possibility of Happy Endings.

Sachs hymns Art as a 'noble illusion' that transforms the mess of human experience into the material of redemption.

WAHN remained an important idea to Wagner throughout the rest of his life.

Holy German Art & Wahn

When he came to build his family house at Bayreuth (1873–74), the name engraved above the door was

WAHNFRIED.

'Peace from Folly' Given what took place there, it acquired a certain irony.

THE MASTERSINGERS is a solid, well-upholstered piece that runs for at least four hours and belies Wagner's declared intention to write 'something lighter'. The score is itself a work of consolidation–as richly expressive as TRISTAN but less chromatically coloured, more traditionally tonal, with an affirmative C major ending.

Where Wagner's new concept of musical drama advocated long, unbroken lines of music 'through-composed' – UNENDLICHE MELODIE – *The Mastersingers* tends towards self-contained numbers. And much of it glows with nostalgia for the music of the past . . .

AFFECTIONATE PARODIES OF BAROQUE COUNTERPOINT AND LUTHERAN CHORALES. . . .

But then, the message of the piece **is** cultural consolidation.

Walther's art succeeds when it looks to the future without ignoring the lessons of the past,when its innovative genius is tempered by agreed form.

The dark side of **THE MASTERSINGERS** is its open invitation to cultural bigotry and undertone of anti-Semitism. Sachs's hymn to Holy German Art can, of itself, read harmlessly enough as a response to topical concerns: the cultural coherence of the German people WAS vulnerable, and WAS periodically under specific threat from France.

But all too easily it yields a more aggressive reading; which is why, for a later Nazi generation, it became a classic statement of **Teutonic Aryan supremacy**:

"Beware! Evil threatens us.
If Germman Folk should one
day fall to foreign rule,
no prince will understand
his people any more, and
foreign vanities will
flourish in our land.

Therefore I say, honour your
German Masters; and then
if the Holy Roman Empire
should dissolve in mist for
us there would remain a
holy German art."

AH, NOW YOU HEAR IT: .A LOOP-HOLE FOR INCOMPETENTS WHO FOLLOW THEIR OWN COURSES AS THEY PLEASE... .ADMITTANCE HERE IS BY THE RULES.

There's no explicit anti-Semitism in **THE MASTERSINGERS**, but the character of Beckmesser has all the qualities that Wagner and his literary mentors identified with Jews.
Coupled with cryptic references to Judaism in the libretto, it is clear enough to most Wagner scholars that Beckmesseris an archetype of the Jewish pseudo-artist who gets his come-uppance.

At the same time, though, Beckmesser is a parody of a particular critic whose pen had wounded Wagner once too often: the leading German music commentator of his time

Eduard Hanslick (1825 - 1904).

THE PROBLEM WITH WAGNER AS A DRAMATIST WAS THAT HIS PLOTS ARE TOO OBVIOUSLY PREDETERMINED. CHARACTERS' "WHO MUST" ARE LESS INTERESTING THAN CHARACTERS WHO OPERATE WITH FREE CHOICE.

Hanslick, like Beckmesser, was a proponent of the old rules of musical form and damning of Wagner's innovations— although in fairness to him, he did acknowledge the essential genius behind them.

The first performance of **THE MASTERSINGERS** took place in Munich (Wagner had been allowed back) at the command of Ludwig; and the conductor was none other than **Hans von Bülow** whose adulation of Wagner survived, undiminished, the fact that the composer had stolen his wife.

'THIS GLORIOUS, UNIQUE MAN WHOM ONE CAN ONLY VENERATE LIKE A GOD'

I COULDN'T AGREE MORE

Ludwig proved less forgiving. Late in 1868, Cosima von Bülow 'officially' took up residence at Tribschen and Ludwig was 'officially' notified. He didn't see Wagner again for eight years - although he continued to pay the bills.

Cosima

From then on, Cosima assumed a central role in the domestic opera of Wagner's life –to the extent that she is probably the most celebrated musical consort in history. She had always moved in musical circles. Her father, *Franz Liszt* had been one of Wagner's greatest champions, until the affair with Cosima began and things turned sour.

24 years younger than Wagner, she became his disciple, servant and – in 1870 after divorcing Hans von Bülow – wife.

Her diaries, in 21 volumes, which record the minutiae of Wagner's life at Tribschen and Bayreuth and which were initially written to justify her marital irregularities to her children, are classic documents:

"My union with Richard is a reincarnation which brings me nearer to perfection, a deliverance,, from a previously erring life

Self-abasement.

Today, children, I committed a grave wrong; I offended our friend . . something I never wish to do again, considering it the blackest of sins. We were speaking of Beethoven's C Minor symphony, and I wilfully insisted on a tempo which I felt to be right.

This astonished and offended R, and now we are both suffering . . . I for having done it, he for having experienced wilfulness at my hands.

I ask him whether I should read Schopenhauer. He advises me against it: a woman should approach philosophy through a man, a poet.

I am in complete agreement.

Wagner is commonly referred to in her diaries as *the Friend* It might almost be *the Lord,* as religious imagery permeates the text.

The Friend has given me the golden pen with which he wrote Tristan and Siegfried, and I consecrate it to these communications. Thus I signify how sacredly I regard the work.

Cosima outlived Wagner by nearly half a century – she died in 1930 – and spent those years as the queen of Bayreuth, controlling its artistic life and fighting off suggestions that the operas should be done in any manner other than

"as Richard wanted".

But in 1869 this was all a long way off.
The immediate issue was…

TRISTAN, THE MASTERSINGERS and everything that happened to Wagner in their wake was merely time out from the supreme task that dominated his life during the 1850s, 60s and 70s. It was THE RING.

To give it its full title THE RING OF THE NIBELUNG

THE RHINEGOLD . THE VALKYRIE

Wagner planned them in the ancient Greek tradition of a three–instalment tragic drama prefaced by a lighter Satyr-play, reflecting the structure of Aeschylus's ORESTEIA.
RHINEGOLD, the 'Satyr-play', is shorter and brighter in tone than the others. It serves as a fantasy prelude — a dungeons–and–dragons story of gods, giants, dwarves and magic gold— to what becomes a dynastic soap opera, scanning the emotions and dilemmas of a proto-human family through succeeding generations.

But RHINEGOLD is only short by comparison with what follows. The rest of THE RING operas increase progressively in length to TWILIGHT OF THE GODS, which has a standard running time of six hours (including intervals) and a First Act longer in itself than the entirety of LA BOHÈME or TOSCA.

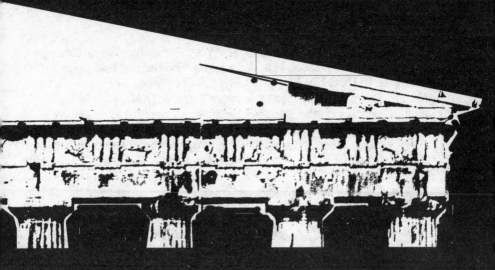

With a total 15 or so hours of music, THE RING is easily the largest theatre piece in history.

is a sequence of four operas, intended to be played on four successive nights:

SIEGFRIED . TWILIGHT OF THE GODS
aka GÖTTERDÄMMERUNG

To stage or even just to see it is a considerable undertaking, illustrative of what Wagner meant when he said his '**artworks of the future**' would not be everyday operatic repertory but special, 'festival' events of national significance – a great public ritual to inspire and regenerate society at large. In the event, THE RING was an epic project that ran away with itself and, as it grew, involved Wagner in a by now familiar pattern of epic problems.

Naturally, the cycle would take place in a purpose-built temple of culture…with specially-trained singers who took <u>no fee</u> (there was to be a dedicated Wagner Academy)…but did it for the <u>honour of involvement</u>…(as was the case at the first cycle in 1876)

                                                            …That, anyway, was the idea.

Essentially THE RING is a myth of Wagner's own devising, although it draws on medieval sources, especially a 13th Century epic poem called the **NIBELUNGENLIED,** which had recently been rediscovered and hailed by German Romantics as a sort of Teutonic ILIAD. Wagner was careful to give his libretto a sense of antiquity by writing it in an archaic verse form known as STABREIM— long sequences of short lines, with a cantering energy derived not from end–rhymes but from internal alliteration. For example (in Stewart Spencer's English translation):

> *LOVELESS HUSBAND,*
> *MOST HEARTLESS OF MEN!*
> *FOR THE BARREN BAUBLE*
> *OF MIGHT AND DOMINION*
> *YOU'D GAMBLE AWAY,*
> *WITH UNGODLY CONTEMPT,*
> *LOVE AND WOMANHOOD'S WORTH.*

Wagner clearly had a high regard for his libretti as artworks in their own right, and took great care to write his music in a way that would support and not obscure the texts.

Like all his mature operas, THE RING uses a massive orchestra whose role is no less important than that of the singers. But Wagner is not just a vast orchestral noise though which words occasionally filter. Nietzsche was closer to the truth when he paradoxically called Wagner

A 'MUSICAL MINIATURIST''

Despite its scale, THE RING is written with the detail and particularity of chamber music. Every small shade of expression registers — and is intended to be heard.

On the opening night of the first complete RING cycle in 1876, Wagner pinned up a notice backstage:

A LAST REQUEST TO MY FAITHFUL ARTISTS!
DISTINCTNESS !

Before we begin, it might help to study

the RING,

a (dysfunctional) family tree

key:

-ꝑ- marriage   ~ coupling   —— offspring

A MORTAL WOMAN~~~~~
(of no fixed address)
(Wotan in wolf's disguise)

the WÄLSUNGS
(A VERY PUT UPON RACE, AMONG WHOM ARE THE SIBLINGS...)

HUNDING-ꝑ-
(a nasty bit of work)

SIEGLINDE~~SIEGMUND
(a tormented housewife)
(a tormented outlaw and also Sieglinde's brother)

the NIBELUNGS

ALBERICH~~GRIMHILD -ꝑ- GIBICH
(nasty & vertically challenged)
the GIBICHUNGS

MIME
(Alberichs brother nastier still, and V.C.)

GUTRUNE -ꝑ- SIEGFRIED~
(well-meaning, muddled, past-it, 'County' type)
(nice lad, rather dim)

GUNTHER-ꝑ-
(an upper crust twit, head of the house of Gibich)

HAGEN
Alberich's boy, (the **nastiest** bit of work, not to be confused with ice–cream)

The RHINEMAIDENS: WOGLINDE, WELLGUNDE....

(Chairman of several Boards)

WOTAN

FRICKA
(Mr. Wotan, Goddess of Marriage, not of Wisdom)

FREIA, FROH & DONNER
(Wotan's ' live–in'–laws)

LOGE (Local Fire Dept.)

FAFFNER & FASHOLT
(Builders offering good terms)

ERDA
(Earthmother, a real goer & Goddess of Wisdom, of course)

~~~~~~~~~~~~

SOME GOD
(OR OTHER)...

the NORNS
(who retell the story at the start of part four)

No.1 NORN
(things past)

No.2 NORN
(things present)

No.3 NORN
(Xmas yet to come)

THE VALKYRIES
(very mobile, noisy necrophiliacs, and every last one of them, Siegfried's AUNT)

BRÜNNHILDE &
her sisters. . .

WALTRAUTE , SCHWERTLEITE
GERHILDE . ORTLINE . ROSSWEISSE
HELMWIGE . GRIMGERDE . SIEGRUNE

....and FLOSSHILDE ('FLOSSY' to her friends)

THE RHINEGOLD or DAS RHEINGOLD (1851-56)

is where the story starts --
--- with a musical idea that Wagner intended to represent the ....

The stage and auditorium are dark; and out of the blackness issues a deep sound of a low E flat from the double basses, gradually rising through the orchestra in an E flat chord that stays fixed in the music for the next fifty bars. One of the great prolonged musical moments in opera.   It casts an extraordinary magic and introduces. . .

. . .the Rhinemaidens swimming in the river. . .

. . .and guarding the Rhinegold.

beginning of the world'.

According to the lore, anyone who renounces love and forges a ring from the gold will become all-powerful—. which happens to be the very objective of the Nibelung dwarf **Alberich**, who curses love, steals the gold, makes THE RING and creates for himself an empire based on the labour and misery of others.

This is of some concern to the gods who have imperial objectives of their own. Wotan, the king of the gods and the main character in THE RING CYCLE has hired two giants Fafner and Fasholt to build him and his family a glittering home, Valhalla. The agreed price is that the giants will take away the goddess Freia as a wife.

THAT'S BIGAMY ON A BIG SCALE!

But after the pressure is put on by Fricka, Wotan breaks the agreement – which was, after all, tough on Freia – and is forced to offer an alternative: the RING OF THE NIBELUNG, which Wotan duly steals from Alberich.

CURSES !!!

Nibelheim

Alberich curses the Ring... and the troubles start.

No sooner have the giants received it in payment than they fight, and one of them is killed.

The gods meanwhile ritually progress across the rainbow bridge to Valhalla with a confidence in their future which is tragically unjustified. As Loge, the fire-bringer, and 'Mr. Fixit' of Valhalla, confides to the audience:

THEY ARE HASTENING TO THEIR END.

CURTAIN.

RHINEGOLD was written to be performed without a break between the scenes (technically it's all contained within a single act) and with nothing to hide the scene changes. Just as the music grows organically out of that opening E flat and progresses (as it were) in one great breath towards the final notes, so the spectacle of the piece was intended to emerge out of the darkness and transform from one scene to the next before the audience's eyes. Wagner said…

THE ART OF COMPOSITION IS THE ART OF TRANSITION!!

As such, this was the first piece to incorporate the ideals of the essay OPERA AND DRAMA, and the first to make real use of recurring motifs as part of the musical structure as well as dramatic signalling. The audience hears fragments of music associated with, for example…

THE RHINEGOLD,

VALHALLA,

etc.

THE CURSE ON LOVE

These will return again in the other RING operas as part of a purely musical commentary on what happens on the stage.

The Valkyrie is where the story really starts –
shifting from the fanciful world of the gods
to the distinctly earthy dimension
of humankind.

Time has passed, **Wotan** has grown wiser, and
come to rue the mistakes he made about **the Ring**.

I NEED TO GET IT BACK TO THE RHINEMAIDENS.
BUT BEING BOUND BY MY OWN LAWS, I CANT
MYSELF EXTRACT IT FROM FAFNER
WHAT SHOULD I DO?
I'LL SEEK AVICE
FROM ERDA.

ONLY AN 'INNOCENT' HERO
ACTING INDEPENDENTLY
CAN DO THE JOB.

THE VALKYRIE

- or DIE VALKÜRE (1851/56)

Wotan has fathered on earth two siblings, Siegmund and Sieglinde, as potential intermediaries. But the plan misfires (the curse of THE RING doing its worst), the siblings are separated as children, and they grow to wretched adulthood: Sieglinde as the slave-wife of a brutal hunter, Hunding, Siegmund as an outlaw.

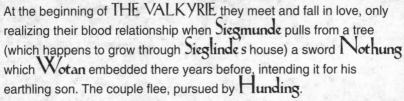

At the beginning of THE VALKYRIE they meet and fall in love, only realizing their blood relationship when Siegmunde pulls from a tree (which happens to grow through Sieglinde's house) a sword Nothung which Wotan embedded there years before, intending it for his earthling son. The couple flee, pursued by Hunding.

At this point the eponymous Valkyrie finally put in an appearance. They are warrior—maidens, fathered by Wotan, whose business it is to recruit dead heroes from earthly battlefields to be the guardians of Valhalla. Wotan's favourite is Brünnhilde.

She is charged to protect Siegmund and Sieglinde on the run.

But **Wotan's** lawful wife, **Fricka**, objects.

SIEGMUND IS COMMITTING INCEST AND BREAKING THE BONDS OF MARRIAGE. . . IT CAN'T BE COUNTENANCED!

Wotan submits, and resigns himself to the fact that

ONLY THE END OF ALL THINGS CAN CLEANSE THE WORLD OF THE MESS THE GODS HAVE CREATED

(A TOUCH OF SCHOPENHAUER'S NIHILISM HERE).

SIEGLINDE SHALL LIVE, AND SIEGMUND BESIDE HER

IT'S DECIDED: I'LL ALTER THE FIGHT.

TO YOU SIEGMUND I'LL GIVE THE ADVANTAGE AND VICTORY

Brünnhilde disobeys (the challenge of love to the rule of power) and tries to save Siegmund.

Wotan intervenes, shatters Siegmund's sword Nothung, and lets him be killed by the avenging husband.

Brünnhilde flees to her sisters

(cue for a musical motif: the Ride of the Valkyries)

with a sorry/ angry **Wotan** in pursuit.

Her punishment is to be divested of divinity and overwhelmed by a magic sleep that leaves her vulnerable to the first man who finds her (she is, needless to say, a virgin).

As a concession of sorts, Wotan surrounds her with a curtain of fire that only a brave hero would dare to penetrate, and with desperate sadness bids his favourite child farewell.

CURTAIN

THE VALKYRIE is probably the easiest point of access to the RING, with vividly created sound worlds for the storm scene at the start, the fire music at the end, and the passionate exchanges of incestuous love in the middle.

That the piece sides with adultery and incest was a shocking matter in its era; but given Wagner's personal circumstances, it speaks from the heart.

He was working on the score at the time of the Wesendonck affair; and his first draft contained no less than 17 coded messages to Mathilde.

Wotan's next attempt at finding an 'innocent' to save the gods from downfall is **Siegfried**, the child of the incestuous union in THE VALKYRIE. Having lost both his parents, he has, by a curious chance, been brought up, in the isolation of a forest cave, by the brother of **Alberich** the dwarf— another equally tricky Nibelung called **Mime**.

114

Mime plans to use Siegfried to kill the giant Fafner (who has by now turned himself into a dragon) and get the Ring– for which purpose he has Siegfried mend the broken pieces of the sword Nothung. Armed with Nothung as was his father before him, and still fearless, Siegfried kills the dragon, claims the Ring,

...and kills Mime whose duplicity has become apparent.

Siegfried then braves the fire
to find Brünnhilde , having first
encountered Wotan
(in disguise) and sliced
his spear in two…

A CRITICAL MANOEUVRE
THAT SIGNALS
SIEGFRIED'S
INDEPENDENCE OF THE
GOD'S DIVINE WILL.

Part of **Siegfried's** innocence is that he's never seen a woman. The discovery of **Brünnhilde** therefore comes as a surprise. That she is technically <u>his aunt</u> is neither here nor there: he kisses her, she wakes, they fall in love.

CURTAIN (slowly)

SIEGFRIED is, in many ways the most problematic of the RING operas. It was a problem for Wagner himself in that he reached the end of Act II and broke off composition.

There followed the <u>twelve-year gap</u> in the writing of the cycle filled by *TRISTAN* and *THE MASTERSINGERS* before he began work on Act III.

As a result, the music of SIEGFRIED changes abruptly in mid course and becomes richer, freer, altogether more developed.

The chief difficulty, though, is the central character. He is meant to be the archetype of golden – locked Teutonic youth, aged around 17 and with the unselfconscious, ruddy vigour to make boorish behaviour vaguely acceptable.

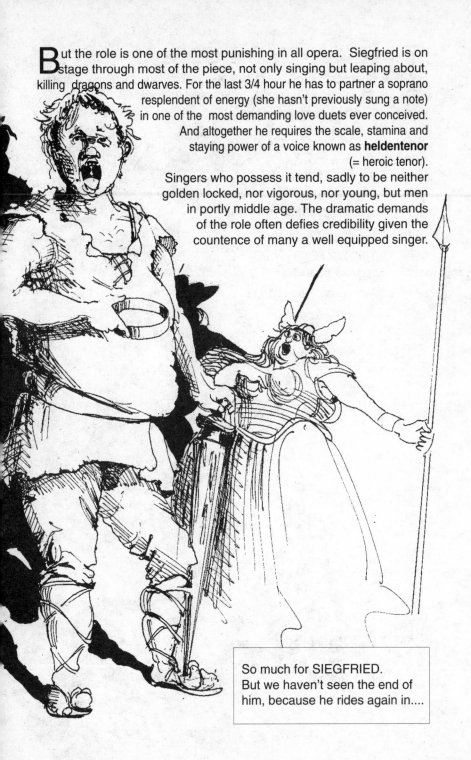

But the role is one of the most punishing in all opera. Siegfried is on stage through most of the piece, not only singing but leaping about, killing dragons and dwarves. For the last 3/4 hour he has to partner a soprano resplendent of energy (she hasn't previously sung a note) in one of the most demanding love duets ever conceived. And altogether he requires the scale, stamina and staying power of a voice known as **heldentenor** (= heroic tenor).

Singers who possess it tend, sadly to be neither golden locked, nor vigorous, nor young, but men in portly middle age. The dramatic demands of the role often defies credibility given the countence of many a well equipped singer.

So much for SIEGFRIED. But we haven't seen the end of him, because he rides again in....

TWILIGHT OF THE GODS

or Götterdämmerung (1848/74) which brings the cycle – and the whole world as envisaged by Wagner' s imagination – to a spectacularly pyrotechnic end.

Despairing for the future, Wotan has piled logs around Valhalla and sits in Schopenhauerian gloom, waiting for the day when the curse of the Ring will be fulfilled and all his creation engulfed in flames.

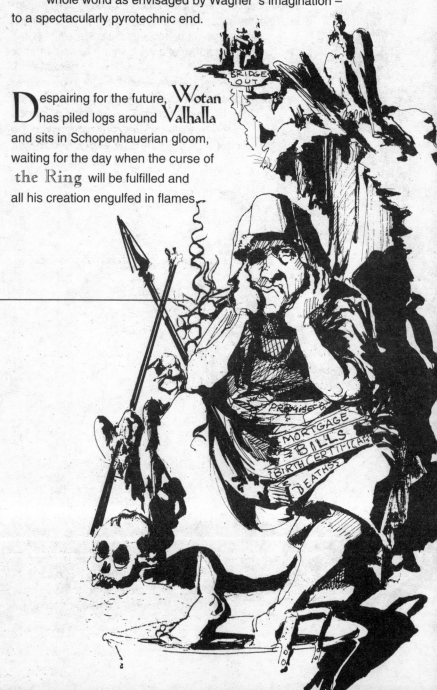

Siegfried journeys down the Rhine. He arrives at the court of Gunther and Gutrune, a malleable brother and sister who rule the land of the Gibichungs under the influence of their half–brother Hagen (a son of the dwarf Alberich and accordingly up to no good).

WHATEVER IT TAKES, GET THE RING

Hagen wants the Ring, and with the use of a disorienting magic potion he persuades Siegfried to betray Brünnhilde and bring her to the court for an enforced marriage to Gunther.

As a reward, Siegfried will be given the hand of Gutrune.

Brünnhilde is so crushed by her betrayal that she reveals to Hagen that his back is the one vulnerable spot on Siegfried's otherwise invincible hero's body, enabling Hagen to kill him and Gunther as well, so as to have sole rights to mastery of the universe.

Having been informed by a desperate Gutrune of the treachery, Brünnhilde builds Siegfried a funeral pyre, declaring that the RING will now – at long last – be returned to the Rhine. As the flames rise, she rides her horse into the fire as a final gesture of self–sacrifice.

At the same time, the waters of the Rhine break their banks and engulf the scene, drowning Hagen as he makes one last desperate attempt to get the Ring.

The waters subside - to reveal that Valhalla itself is ablaze. The era of the gods is over.

CURTAIN

The question at the end of GÖTTERDÄMMERUNG, not unreasonably, is

WHAT DOES IT ALL MEAN?

That no one can definitively say has been a gift for stage directors ever since. Wagner himself had no convincing explanation for much of what he had written.

AN ARTIST IN THE PRESENCE OF HIS OWN WORK IS FACED, IF IT IS GENUINE ART, BY RIDDLES ABOUT WHICH HE TOO MAY BE DECEIVED, LIKE ANYBODY ELSE'

The libretto comes programmed with deliberate ambiguities and conflicts of logic intended to fill out the texture of the piece into something of **true mythic stature.**

Libretto

CHROEOGRAPHY

Scenic design & dimensions

Answers to unasked questions

Stage directions

and swimming

Singers' proportions

References to improve understanding

QUESTIONS TO IMPROVE REFERENCES

Questions never to be asked

For example, the saga's very end. THE RING has been returned to the Rhine, Brünnhilde has sacrificed herself for love, and every conceivable act of Wagnerian redemption / atonement has been observed.

SO WHY DOES VALHALLA STILL BURN? WHY DOES THE WORLD DESTRUCT?

IT IS EMOTIONALLY APPROPRIATE... THE NECESSITY FOR THE DOWNFALL OF THE GODS SPRINGS FROM OUR INNERMOST FEELINGS, AS IT DOES FROM THE INNERMOST FEELINGS OF WOTAN WILLING HIS OWN DOWNFALL!

Having changed the final words of the libretto three times, he settled on a neutral statement that sidesteps any reasoned analysis of what is happening. The one more–or–less unchallengeable reading you could make of the piece is that it is an allegorical history of the world fixed on a course to disaster.

Wagner wrote to Liszt:

Mark my new poem well. It holds the world's beginning and its destruction.

The essence of what goes wrong is that

THE PURSUIT OF LOVE
is compromised
by
THE DESIRE FOR POWER

But beyond that basic idea, readings of THE RING fall broadly into three categories.

(1) THE RING AS A CRITIQUE OF CAPITALISM

This is argued by
George Bernard Shaw
(1856 - 1950), whose celebrated
commentary
The Perfect Wagnerite
understood the cycle as...

A SOCIALIST FABLE ON MATERIAL GREED AS 'THE ROOT OF ALL EVIL.'

This reading stresses Wagner's socio–political commitment, and his interest in the French economic philosopher

Pierre Joseph Proudhon (1809-1865)

whose essay **WHAT IS PROPERTY?**

answered its own question with the reply . . . *PROPERTY IS THEFT.*

Proudhon argued that capitalism was the natural enemy of love, and love the true goal of mankind.

(2) THE RING AS SCHOPENHAUERIAN PESSIMISM

Wotan acts as a personification of the Will of the world, trained inexorably on **self–destruction**.

Wagner actually knew nothing of Schopenhauer's work when THE RING libretto was first published, but it proved such a powerful discovery that it changed Wagner's reading of his own words when he came to set them.

(3) THE RING AS EXPLORATION

This is the Freudian-cum-Jungian interpretation championed by the musicologist Robert Donington and taking as its starting point Wagner's claim (in **OPERA AND DRAMA**) that it was the function of the artist...

TO BRING THE UNCONSCIOUS PART OF HUMAN NATURE ——————— *INTO CONSCIOUSNESS.*

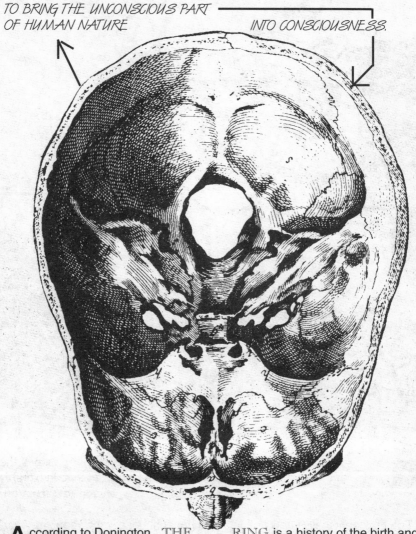

According to Donington, THE RING is a history of the birth and development of consciousness, expressed in imagery closely linked to that of biblical creation myths.

OF THE PSYCHE

Emerging from the waters of oblivion, consciousness comes with the predetermined event of the stealing of the Ring: a reflection of what medieval theologians called the 'fortunate fall' of Eve stealing the apple, and a necessary rite of passage from nature to culture.

Thereafter, Donington takes all the characters of THE RING as parties to a drama of the workings of the mind, with Alberich and Wotan as conflicting aspects of the same internal energy

...a **yin** and **yang**.

In the course of the text Wotan does actually refer to himself as 'light Alberich' and to the dwarf as 'black', suggesting some kind of relationship that binds them through their opposition.

Interpreting THE RING encourages speculative sophistication, but **STAGING** it requires a degree of practicality to which the piece has always been resistant.

I KNEW FROM THE START THAT I NEEDED A SPECIAL THEATRE, THE LIKE OF WHICH DOES NOT EXIST. IT WOULD HAE TO BUILT TO ORDER.

He envisaged a temporary wooden structure initially in Zurich, then Munich, and finally **BAYREUTH**.

WHERE?

This was a small to middling town in Bavaria which became the international focus of Wagner activity.

B ut it took years to raise the money (from subscribers, from Wagner societies around the world, from Cosima's inheritance and, of course, from Ludwig).

Meanwhile, the first two operas from THE RING cycle had indivdual premières in Munich – greatly to Wagner's annoyance.

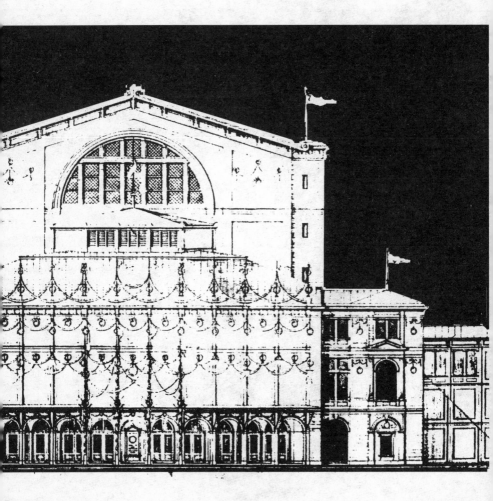

Never less than opportunist, Wagner turned to Bismarck and the German Emperor, offering to make Bayreuth a symbol for German unification.

Bismarck wasn't interested. In anger, Wagner threatened to emigrate to Minnesota where a community of German–American Wagnerites had promised him the theatre of his dreams.

In the end, the **BAYREUTH FESTSPIELHAUS** (festival playhouse) opened with the first ever cycles of THE RING in August 1876: a great social event attended by the Emperor, Liszt, Tchaikovsky and Ludwig, who pointedly failed to show until the third cycle.

Tchaikovsky noted of the festival environment...

...CUTLETS, BAKED POTATOES, OMELETTES ARE MORE ENTHUSIASTICALLY DISCUSSED THAN THE MUSIC OF WAGNER

But Wagner had his theatre—a 'temproary' structure, built largely of wood, and still standing more than a century later as a monument to his theatrical vision.

Designed like a Greek amphitheatre, as opposed to the horseshoe auditorium with tiers of boxes which was usual for the time, it reflects the Wagnerian ideal of theatre as a quasi-religious communal activity rather than an entertainment.

The audience sit, without hierarchic division, in a fan-shaped block. When the lights go down, the doors are locked (with a fire engine outside in case of emergency) to prevent disturbance.

The theatre is now in total darkness – because the orchestra pit digs deep under the stage and is screened by a hood that (a) prevents the orchestra from overwhelming the singers, and (b) hides the orchestra from view.

There is a cunning trick of perspective: a double proscenium that seems to extend towards the audience by means of a row of false proscenium pillars on each side of the auditorium. Wagner's intention was that…

THE SPECTATOR HAS THE FEELING OF BEING AT A FAR DISTANCE FROM EVENTS ON STAGE, YET PERCEIVES THEM WITH A CLARITY OF NEAR PROXIMITY; IN CONSEQUENCE, THE STAGE FIGURES SEEM TO BE *ENLARGED* AND *SUPERHUMAN!*

From a purely human point of view, not everything about the FESTSPIELHAUS is perfect. It wasn't designed for comfort: the seats are hard (sleep if you dare) and the temperature asphyxiating. People occasionally collapse (and even die) propped up in their places until the doors are opened.

Bayreuth proved to be an enormous influence on the conduct of modern theatre. It endowed the idea of **performance** with a hallowed seriousness of purpose and set new standards for the dramatization of music.

What the audiences actually see at Bayreuth, though, has come to be a matter of ENDURING CONTROVERSY. Wagner provided specific, and copious, instructions for the staging of THE RING and envisaged the realistic portrayal of spectacular events without actually explaining how to do them. The cycle opens with Rhinemaidens swimming underwater and closes with a flood and fire in rapid succession. In between…

THE GODDESS FRICKA ENTERS ON A CHARIOT DRAWN BY RAMS,

AND ALBERICH TRANSFORMS INTO A TOAD.

THIS CONTRACT SAYS TOAD... IT DOESNT SAY SHRINK !

SIEGFRIED PLAYS WITH A BEAR AND FIGHTS A DRAGON,

BRUNNHILDE RIDES HER HORSE INTO A FLAMING PYRE,

It's hardly surprising that Wagner was disappointed with the way the first cycles looked. But he stood by a naturalistic approach; and so did Cosima when she took control of Bayreuth after his death.

In fact, she fossilized Wagner staging into the routines of horn-helmeted Valkyries and shaggy, skin–clad Siegfrieds bounding through forest clearings which are now consigned to comedy.

THE RING WAS PERFORMED HERE IN 1876; CONSEQUENTLY, IN RESPECT OF SCENERY AND STAGING, THERE IS NOTHING MORE TO BE DISCOVERED.

PHFEW!

the one and only way to play is Richard's way!

145

I t remained much the same after her death in 1930, when Wagner's English–born daughter–in–law **Winifred** (1897–1980) took over and proved resistant to innovation. Winifred Williams married Wagner's son Siegfried in 1915 and proved to be the **serious Nazi** in the Wagner clan, (together with Wagner's son–in–law, Houston Stewart Chamberlain, also English-born!)

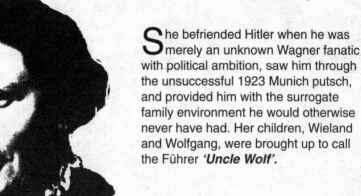

S he befriended Hitler when he was merely an unknown Wagner fanatic with political ambition, saw him through the unsuccessful 1923 Munich putsch, and provided him with the surrogate family environment he would otherwise never have had. Her children, Wieland and Wolfgang, were brought up to call the Führer *'Uncle Wolf'*.

die Stadt Richard Wagners
grüßt die Gäste des Führers

In return, Hitler enshrined Bayreuth as a Nazi temple of culture and adopted Wagner's music as the soundtrack to the Third Reich.

None of this did Wagner any favours when the Second World War ended.

From 1945/ 51 Bayreuth was closed down by the Allies for a period of **'decontamination'**.

When it reopened, *Wieland Wagner*
(1917–1966)

was in charge and concerned (to borrow
a Wagnerian term) to redeem Bayreuth
from its past. There was a clean break
with the old style of presentation .

OUT WENT NORDIC SAGA DECOR –
THE BREASTPLATES, BEARSKINS,
SAGGING TIGHTS, AND ANY IDEA
OF THE RING AS A CELEBRATION
OF THE GERMAN VOLK . . .

…in came simple, stripped–
bare stagings, based on light
projections and THE RING
as universal property.

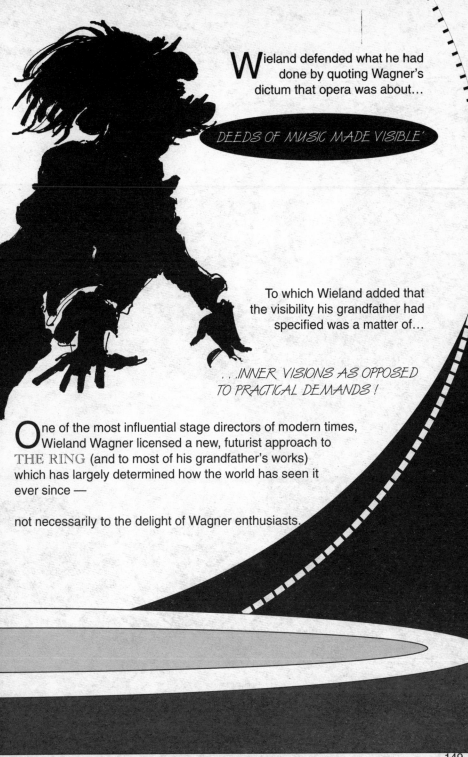

Wieland defended what he had done by quoting Wagner's dictum that opera was about...

'DEEDS OF MUSIC MADE VISIBLE'

To which Wieland added that the visibility his grandfather had specified was a matter of...

...INNER VISIONS AS OPPOSED TO PRACTICAL DEMANDS !

One of the most influential stage directors of modern times, Wieland Wagner licensed a new, futurist approach to THE RING (and to most of his grandfather's works) which has largely determined how the world has seen it ever since —

not necessarily to the delight of Wagner enthusiasts.

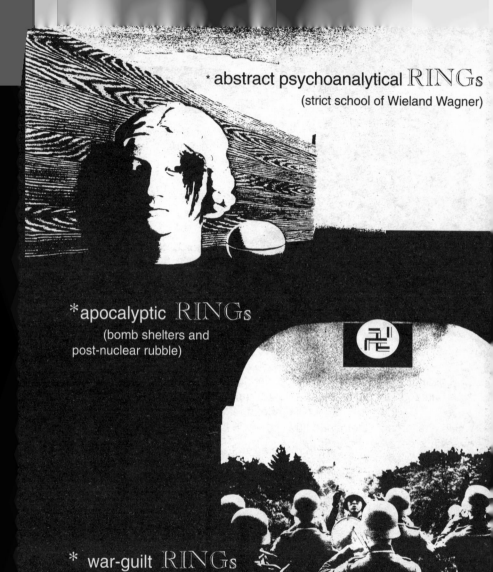

* abstract psychoanalytical RINGs
(strict school of Wieland Wagner)

*apocalyptic RINGs
(bomb shelters and
post-nuclear rubble)

* war-guilt RINGs
(a German speciality,
awash with swastikas)

* space age knockabout

RINGs

(cartoon style, with costumes
filched from faded episodes
of Star Trek)

* anti-capitalist political

RINGs

(smoking jackets and leather armchairs)

The French director Patrice Chereau's
Centenary RING at Bayreuth in 1976
turned Brünnhilde into a 'petroleuse
aristocratique' - a high class terrorist
rebelling against parental oppression.
It was topical at the time.

Perhaps the ultimate in avant garde productions have been
* 'innocent' RINGS that resurrect the Nordic literalism of
l9th Century Bayreuth, complete with bearskins, sagging tights and stick–on pigtails. The innocent approach has probably been the least successful and most vulnerable to the absurdities THE RING, like much great art, encompasses in reaching for the stars.

There can be no going back. As Wagner said himself to subsequent interpreters...

CHILDREN, DO SOMETHING NEW.

THE RING may have been Wagner's greatest achievement but it wasn't his last. There was still to come the most provocative and questionable music drama of all — a piece which **Nietzsche**, that disciple–turned–enemy of the composer called…

AN OUTRAGE ON MORALITY!

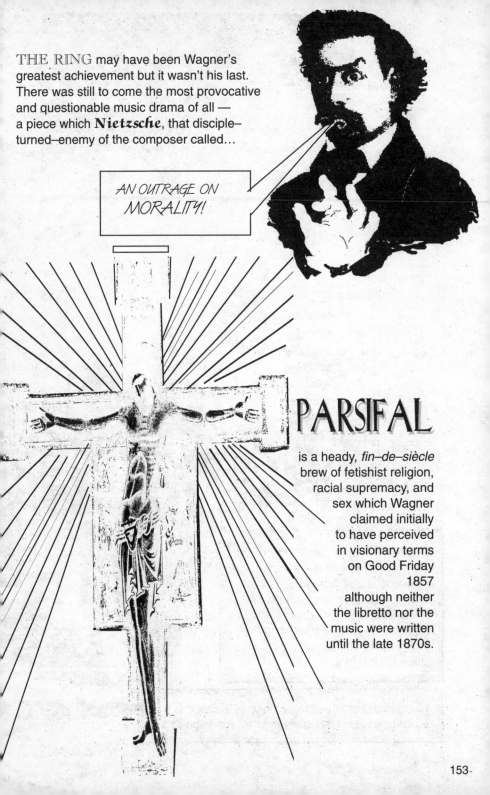

PARSIFAL

is a heady, *fin–de–siècle* brew of fetishist religion, racial supremacy, and sex which Wagner claimed initially to have perceived in visionary terms on Good Friday 1857 although neither the libretto nor the music were written until the late 1870s.

Derived from a 13th Century German Romance, the story concerns a brotherhood of militant monks who guard the Christian relics of the Holy Grail (the chalice used by Jesus at the Last Supper) and the Holy Spear (which pierced his side at the Crucifixion).

Excluded from this brotherhood is Klingsor, a magician who takes revenge for his exclusion ...

In the process of seduction, Amfortas loses the Spear to Klingsor and receives a wound that will not heal.

ONLY A BLAMELESS FOOL MADE WISE THROUGH SUFFERING COMPASSION CAN REDEEM ME.

Parsifal, a youth seeking adventure, is the blameless fool: an innocent, who identifies with the suffering of **Amfortas** and so resists the temptations of **Kundry**, who tries to seduce him by pretending to be his mother (very Wagnerian).

He recovers the Spear and on Good Friday returns it to the chapel of the brotherhood where he heals Amfortas's wound, baptizes a remorseful Kundry, and performs the ritual of the Grail himself.

Redeemed at last from guilt, Kundry falls lifeless to the ground.

CURTAIN.

PARSIFAL, like THE RING, resists definitive interpretation. In one sense it is a parable of sexual asceticism and denial as the open – sesame to salvation and a riposte to *TRISTAN*, which suggests exactly the opposite

It also seems to be a work of Christian art: a medieval mystery play burdened with late 19th Century neuroses.

But Wagner's relationship with Christianity was equivocal. He was always interested in Christian imagery – it passed heavily into TANNHÄUSER and LOHENGRIN – and at one time he sketched a five–act opera to be called JESUS OF NAZARETH; but it was no more than one of the many, varied sources from which he culled and customized ideas.

The real roots of PARSIFAL lie – yet again – in Schopenhauer, and his Aryan alignment of Christianity with Buddhism rather than Judaism. At its heart is the ideal of compassion (**MITLEID**) and renunciation: qualities possessed by gentiles, not by Jews, and the means by which PARSIFAL cures the ills of Amfortas and the brotherhood.

It follows, according to some interpreters, that the brotherhood represents true Aryan Christianity undermined by false Jewish Christianity (Klingsor), with Kundry (described by Wagner as a variant on the Wandering Jew) as a communicating channel between them that must be claimed and silenced.

Whatever Wagner meant, he certainly invested PARSIFAL with sacred significance. It was designated a BÜHNENWEHFESTSPIEL a stage-festival-consecration-play. As part of the aura of sacredness, performances were for the next 30 years limited by deed of law to Bayreuth – which meant that Cosima spent the next 30 years challenging, sabotaging and otherwise denouncing pirate productions

It was also one of the concluding ironies of Wagner's life that this most Aryan of artworks was premièred in July 1882 by a Jewish conductor (Hermann Levi, the son of a Rabbi), with a Jewish designer and Jewish stage manager. Wagner bitterly objected; but by now he had surrendered all rights in his works to Ludwig in return for paying off Bayreuth's accumulated debts. Adding insult to accumulated injury, Ludwig was now in love with a young Jewish actor.

In 1886, **King Ludwig II** of **Bavaria** was officially declared insane and deposed.

Five days later he was discovered drowned in Lake Starnberg, outside Munich.

A memorial cross rises out of the water to mark the spot.

Seven months later, Wagner was in Venice.

On the morning of 13 February 1883 he had an argument with Cosima about a Flower – maiden called Carrie Pringle.

In the afternoon, in bed, writing an essay on

'The Eternal Feminine in Humanity',

he had a heart attack and died.

So much of Wagner's life and work seems disagreeable that his greatness as an artist doesn't readily reduce to words.
Direct experience of the music is what counts, bypassing logic and reason just as it was meant to. Wagner's strength and weakness was the driven, single-minded quality of his ambition – to encompass epic projects on the grandest scale.
It may seem at times a kind of madness; but one empowered by genius that saw his visions through, against all odds.

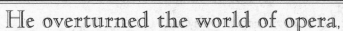

He overturned the world of opera,

stretching the old forms to create a new genre of work,
a symphonic drama, that demanded...

* **a new kind of singer**

(the Wagnerian voice: heavy, huge, and with far greater
staying power than voices ever needed for a Mozart aria)

* **a new expanded orchestra**

(with instruments like the Wagner tuba, double bassoon and bass
trumpet which had never before been seen, or heard, in an opera pit)

* a new kind of theatre to house them

(the Festspielhaus has influenced modern theatre design, based on dynamics and the physics of sound more than on decor and comfort)

* a new kind of music

(Wagner stretched traditional harmony and tonality to a breaking point, and pointed the way to a *new music*, first, via Anton Bruckner and Gustav Mahler's symphonies, and then to Modernist Expressionism and the atonality of Alban Berg, Arnold Schoenberg and Anton von Webern).

For many listeners – and for the early 20th century composers he inspired – Wagner is where modern music begins. For others, like the critic **Eduard Hanslick**, his excesses make him a terminal rather than a founding figure…

> WAGNER'S ART RECOGNIZES ONLY SUPERLATIVES, AND A SUPERLATIVE HAS NO FUTURE. IT IS AN END, NOT A BEGINNING . . .
>
> WHEN ART ENTERS A PERIOD OF LUXURY IT IS IN DECLINE.

But the power of Wagner is such that it has always been possible to despise his personality and ideas and still be captivated by the music, as **Nietzsche** was…

> I DECLARE WAGNER TO HAVE BEEN THE GREATEST BENEFACTOR OF MY LIFE.

To be victim of his ideas and still love the music, as many Jews do. Mahler and Schoenberg are only two examples. And there are plenty of listeners who claim actively to dislike the music but remain obsessed by it, among them **Claude Debussy**….

> THAT OLD POISONER !

Wagner's venom was in fact, like all his other qualities, ambivalent. **Paul Hindemith**, composer (1895–63), perceived its uses.

> NOT UNTIL THE TURN OF THE CENTURY DID THE OUTLINES OF THE NEW WORLD DISCOVERED IN TRISTAN BEGIN TO TAKE SHAPE. MUSIC REACTED TO IT AS A HUMAN BODY TO AN INJECTED SERUM WHICH IT STRIVES TO EXCLUDE AND ONLY AFTERWARDS LEARNS TO ACCEPT AS NECESSARY AND EVEN WHOLESOME.

Wagner ... wholesome?

If you want to be in fashion, you must refer darkly to the evil workings of the RING in the Teutonic mentality – though as the whole cycle of operas is devoted to showing that even the gods can't break an agreement without bringing the whole universe crashing about their ears...

I've never been able to see what possible encouragement Hitler can have got out of it.

(Edmund Crispin: SWAN SONG)

CURTAIN!

WAGNER CHRONOLOGY

1813 Wilhelm Richard Wagner born Leipzig 22 May.

1814 His mother Johanna Rosine marries Ludwig Geyer and family moves to Dresden.

1821 After Ludwig Geyer's death, Wagner boards with his stepfather's brother Carl in Eisleben.

1822–26 Attends Kreuzschule, Dresden, as Wilhelm Richard Geyer. Shows interest in ancient mythology and music. Remains in Dresden when his mother and sisters move to Prague. There his sister Rosalie begins her stage career.

1828 After rejoining his family in Leipzig, attends the Nikolai Gymnasium, reassuming the name Wagner. Studies composition with Christian Gottlieb Müller.

1830 After leaving Nikolai Gymnasium, attends the Thomasschule in Leipzig.

1831 Studies music at Leipzig University for a time. Studies composition with Christian Theodor Weinlig, Cantor at the Thomasschule.

1832 Works on many compositions, including his first opera *Die Hochzeit*, which he later abandons. Travels to Vienna and Prague, where his Symphony in C major is performed, and returns to Leipzig.

1833 Begins work on his first completed opera *Die Feen*. Symphony in C major is performed in Leipzig. Employed as chorus master at Würzburg theatre.

1834 Completes *Die Feen*. Leaves his post at Würzburg and returns to Leipzig where he begins work on his next opera *Das Liebesverbot*. While working as musical director of a travelling theatre company at Lauchstädt, he meets the actress Minna Planer. Appointed musical director at Magdeburg theatre.

1836 *Das Liebesverbot* is completed and performed for the first time at Magdeburg. Travels to Königsberg in search of work and marries Minna Planer, who is performing there.

1837 Obtains post as musical director at Königsberg theatre. Begins libretto of *Rienzi*. To escape creditors, flees to Riga, where he takes up post as conductor and is joined by Minna.

1838 Completes libretto and begins composing *Rienzi*. Conducts several of his own works at successful series of concerts at Riga.

1839 Sacked from his post as conductor and hounded by creditors again, crosses border into Russia, together with Minna and their Newfoundland dog Robber, and sails for London. After a short stay, travels to France and takes up lodgings in Paris. Meets Giacomo Meyerbeer for the first time.

1840 Debts force him into musical hack work and journalism, but he manages to complete *Rienzi*. First meeting with Franz Liszt.

1841 On Meyerbeer's recommendation, Dresden Opera accept *Rienzi*. Completes *Der fliegende Holländer*.

1842 Leaves Paris for Dresden and visits family in Leipzig. Begins work on *Tannhäuser*. First performance of *Rienzi* in Dresden is a great success.

1843 Directs the first performance of *Der fliegende Holländer* at Dresden. Appointed conductor of the Dresden court opera.

1845 *Tannhäuser* completed and performed under Wagner at the Dresden court theatre. Begins work on *Die Meistersinger von Nürnberg* and *Lohengrin*.

1846 Meets Hans von Bülow for the

first time. Receives large grant from Dresden opera authorities enabling him to pay off his debts.

1848 Wagner's mother dies aged 74. Completes *Lohengrin* and begins work on the libretti of *Der Ring des Nibelungen* and *Götterdämmerung*.

1849 Takes part in Dresden uprising and forced to flee first to Liszt in Weimar then into exile in Switzerland, where Minna eventually joins him. Writes essays *The Art-work of the Future* and *Art and Revolution*.

1850 Love affair with Jessie Laussot in Bordeaux ends with his return to Minna in Zurich. His essay *Judaism in Music* is published anonymously. At Weimar, Liszt produces the first performance of *Lohengrin* which the exiled Wagner cannot attend.

1851 Writes *Opera and Drama* and the autobiographical *A Communication to My Friends* and completes the first version of the poem for *Siegfried*.

1852 Meets Otto and Mathilde Wesendonck. Completes the first versions of the poems for *Die Walküre* and *Das Rheingold* and reads all four poems of *Der Ring des Nibelungen* to friends at Zürich.

1853 Composes a polka and a piano sonata for Mathilde Wesendonck and begins composing *Das Rheingold*. In Paris sees Liszt's daughter Cosima, then aged 16, for first time.

1854 Begins composing *Die Walküre* and finishes *Das Rheingold*.

1855 Travels to London where he conducts eight concerts popular with audiences but not with music critics.

1856 Completes *Die Walküre*. The first act is performed privately on Liszt's birthday, with Liszt at the piano and Wagner singing several parts. Begins composing *Siegfried*.

1857 Moves into Asyl, villa on Wesendonck estate near Zürich. Hans von Bülow and Cosima Liszt are married and spend part of honeymoon with Wagners. Completes first version of poem for *Tristan und Isolde* and gives it to Mathilde Wesendonck with whom he is in love. Begins composing *Tristan und Isolde*. Also composes a cycle of lieder, settings of poems by Mathilde. Their relationship imposes increasing strains on his marriage and leads to a separation from Minna, who leaves for Germany. Wagner travels to Geneva and Venice where he continues to work on *Tristan und Isolde*.

1859 Travels to Milan and Lucerne, where, after several visits to the Wesendoncks, he completes *Tristan und Isolde*. To further plans for a performance of *Tannhäuser*, Wagner travels to Paris, where he is joined by Minna. He conducts three concerts featuring music from his operas and attended by Berlioz, Meyerbeer, Auber and Gounod. After receiving a partial amnesty, travels through Germany, eventually returning to Paris with Minna. Writes essay *Music of the Future* and begins rehearsing *Tannhäuser* at Paris Opéra. After three performances, he withdraws it because of hostile reception. Attends performance of *Lohengrin* at Vienna and receives ovation.

1862 Moves to Biebrich, where he is briefly joined by Minna. Granted full amnesty by King of Saxony. Resumes work on *Die Meistersinger von Nürnberg*. Visited by Hans and Cosima von Bülow. Conducts *Lohengrin* for the first time at Frankfurt. Visits Minna in Dresden and they finally separate.

1863 Conducts series of successful concerts during tours of main cities of

Austro-Hungary, Germany and Russia. Moves to Penzing, near Vienna. Spends extravagantly on luxurious furnishings for new home. During visit to the Bülows in Berlin, he and Cosima vow to belong to each other only.

1864 Pursued by creditors, but saved from debtors' prison by meeting and subsequent friendship with newly crowned Ludwig II of Bavaria who pays his debts and provides him with income and house. Ludwig commissions *Der Ring des Nibelungen* and appoints Hans von Bülow court pianist. Wagner conducts the first performance of *Der fliegende Holländer* at Munich for Ludwig.

1865 Isolde, Cosima's first child by Wagner, born in April. *Tristan und Isolde*, conducted by Bülow and performed before Ludwig for the first time, is successful with the public but not the press. Their attacks on Wagner force Ludwig to advise him to leave Munich and he moves to Switzerland.

1866 Minna Wagner dies in Dresden in January. At Ludwig's expense, Wagner moves into Tribschen by Lake Lucerne, where he is visited by Hans and Cosima von Bülow, separately and together, and by Ludwig. Works on *Die Meistersinger von Nürnberg*.

1867 Second child born to Wagner and Cosima in February. Hans von Bülow is appointed court conductor and director of the Royal Music School. Wagner completes *Die Meistersinger von Nürnberg* and presents score to Ludwig as Christmas gift.

1868 *Die Meistersinger von Nürnberg* receives its first performance at Munich, conducted by Bülow, before Ludwig accompanied by Wagner.

Nietzsche and Wagner meet for the first time. After much toing and froing between her husband and Wagner, Cosima and the children finally settle in Tribschen. Wagner presents *Rienzi* score to Ludwig as Christmas gift.

1869 Returns to composing *Siegfried* after twelve years. Cosima begins her diaries of their life together and gives birth to their third child Siegfried in June. First visit of Nietzsche to Tribschen. Ludwig orders first performance of *Das Rheingold* despite Wagner's objections to the splitting of *Der Ring des Nibelungen*. Works on composition of *Götterdämmerung*.

1870 Ludwig orders first performance of *Die Walküre* again despite Wagner's protests. Wagner and Cosima are married in August after her divorce from Hans von Bülow in July. Composes *Siegfried Idyll* which is performed at Tribschen for Cosima on her thirty-third birthday.

1871 Completes *Siegfried*. Conducts concert in Berlin before the German Emperor. Plans to build his own theatre at Bayreuth for which town council donate land.

1872 Moves to Bayreuth. Lays foundation stone of theatre and conducts performance of Beethoven's Ninth Symphony at ceremony. Liszt visits Bayreuth.

1873 Reads poem of *Götterdämmerung* to friends and patrons in Berlin and conducts concerts there and at Hamburg and Cologne. Bruckner visits Bayreuth and dedicates his Third Symphony to Wagner.

1874 Ludwig provides financial backing for the building of the Bayreuth theatre after crisis over lack of funds. Wagner and family move into Haus Wahnfried, their newly built home at

Bayreuth. Under the conductor Hans Richter, the first group of singers begins rehearsing the *Ring* cycle which, as Wagner finishes composing *Götterdämmerung*, is complete 26 years after its inception.

1875 Conducts concerts in Vienna, Budapest and Berlin in aid of the Bayreuth Festspielhaus building fund. Produces and attends performances of *Tannhäuser* and *Lohengrin* conducted by Richter in Vienna.

1876 *Tristan und Isolde* performed in Vienna in aid of the Bayreuth fund. At Bayreuth intensive rehearsals of the *Ring* culminating in a dress rehearsal attended by Ludwig. The joy of Wagner and Cosima over the artistic success of the first performance of the *Ring* cycle at the Festspielhaus, attended by several crowned heads and other leading composers, is marred by its financial failure.

1877 Festspielhaus programme cancelled because of financial problems. Continues composing *Parsifal*. Conducts eight concerts in London and is received at Windsor by Queen Victoria. Returns to Germany and reads *Parsifal* poem to friends at Heidelberg.

1878 Breach between Nietzsche and Wagner. Conducts private performance of *Parsifal* Prelude for first time at Wahnfried.

1879 Continues composing Parsifal. The Festspielhaus programme for 1880 in jeopardy.

1880 Wagner and family in Italy for most of year. Ludwig puts his court orchestra and opera chorus at Wagner's disposal for next Festspielhaus season. At their last meeting, Wagner conducts a performance of the *Parsifal* Prelude at Munich for Ludwig alone. Continues working on *Parsifal*.

1881 Wagner and Cosima attend first performances of the *Ring* in Berlin. Illness delays the completion of *Parsifal*. Wagner and family stay in Italy from late 1881 to early 1882.

1882 Completes *Parsifal* in Palermo in January. Returns to Bayreuth in May for rehearsals of *Parsifal* in Festspielhaus. Hermann Levi and Franz Fischer conduct 16 performances of Parsifal with Wagner conducting the last scene of the final performance.

1883 Wagner dies on 13 February and is buried in the grounds of Wahnfried on 18 February.

1884–1906 Cosima continues as director of the Festspielhaus.

SELECT BIBLIOGRAPHY

John Culshaw, *Reflections on Wagner's Ring* (New York and London, 1976). A short and readable collection of essays (originally broadcast talks) by the record producer responsible for the pioneering Solti *Ring* cycle on Decca.

Robert Donington, *Wagner's Ring and Its Symbols* (London and New York, 1963). The psychological approach: strikingly clever Jungian analysis that raises as many questions as it answers but has steered the thinking of a generation of interpreters.

Geoffrey Skelton (editor), *Cosima Wagner's Diaries* (London, 1994). A masterly single-volume abridgement of the mass of Cosima's daily reflections. Fascinating, horrifying, history-as-it-happened.

Bryan Magee, *Aspects of Wagner* (London, 1968). A very slim book but a modern classic: clear, concise, analysis of Wagner's thinking and a model study of its kind.

Barry Millington (editor) *The Wagner Compendium* (London, 1922). A big, encyclopaedic reference book, impressively wide-ranging and well organized for easy use.

Ernest Newman, *The Life of Richard Wagner* (London, 1947). A massive four-volume study with, in its day, biblical authority. Partisan but still persuasive.

Ernest Newman, *Wagner Nights* (London, 1949, New York, 1950). A blow-by-blow account of the main operas: background, content, implications. *The* essential bedside book for Wagner lovers.

Andrew Porter (translator) *The Ring of the Nibelungs* (London, 1976). The best translation going of Wagner's *Ring* libretti, although there is a strong, scholarly and more recent contender from Stewart Spencer and Barry Millington (London, 1993).

George Bernard Shaw, *The Perfect Wagnerite* (London, 1898). A period classic peddling a strong political agenda. To be read with sceptical affection.

Frederic Spotts, *Bayreuth: A History of the Festival* (New York and London, 1994). Beautifully written, presented and illustrated with just the right balance between passion and detachment to give a fair idea of matters steeped in controversy.

Wolfgang Wagner, *Acts* (London, 1994). A family retrospect by the composer's grandson. Interesting, but don't believe a word of it.

DISCOGRAPHY

Der fliegende Holländer (The Flying Dutchman) Christoph von Dohnányi conducting the Vienna Philharmonic Orchestra on Decca is the strongest recent recording, with a committed Senta in Hildegard Behrens.

Lohengrin Georg Solti conducting the Vienna Philharmonic Orchestra on Decca, with superb soloists in Placido Domingo and Jessye Norman.

Die Meistersinger von Nürnberg (The Mastersingers of Nuremberg) Wolfgang Sawallisch conducting the Bavarian State Orchestra on EMI has to be the best recording all round of modern times, with an unsurpassed Walther in Ben Heppner.

Parsifal Herbert von Karajan conducting the Berlin Philharmonic Orchestra on Deutsche Grammophon (1980, Peter Hofmann in the title role) remains a recommended version. Or more recently there is Domingo and Norman under James Levine, also on DG.

Tannhäuser All the best recordings use the Paris version of the score. Giuseppe Sinopoli on Deutsche Grammophon, with soloists including Domingo and Agnes Baltsa (as Venus) has the edge.

Tristan und Isolde (Tristan and Isolde) Solti conducting the Vienna Philharmonic Orchestra on Decca has the great Wagnerian soprano Birgit Nilsson as Isolde. For a distinguished English language version, try Reginald Goodall (British Wagner conductor, famous for slow speeds) on Decca.

Der Ring des Nibelungen (The Ring of the Nibelung) Solti's complete cycle with the Vienna Philharmonic Orchestra for Decca (1959–65) was a landmark in recording history and is still *the* great set, with a dazzling cast: Birgit Nilsson as Brünnhilde and stars like Hans Hotter, Wolfgang Windgassen, Joan Sutherland, Dietrich Fischer-Dieskau, in other roles. The legendary Kirsten Flagstad came out of retirement to sing Fricka. For a more modern version, Daniel Barenboim's live recordings from Bayreuth on Teldec are impressive and feature the outstanding British bass John Tomlinson as Wotan.

Michael White is one of Britain's best-known opera commentators. He is chief music critic of the *Independent on Sunday* and a regular broadcaster on radio and television.

Kevin Scott is an American-born painter, designer and opera producer, now living near Marlborough. He is co-founder and artistic director of the opera company Opera Inside Out.